D1327875

A WORDSWORTH HANDBOOK

CLASSIC SPORTS CARS

Wordsworth Editions

First published in England 1994 by
Wordsworth Editions Ltd
Cumberland House
Crib Street
Ware
Hertfordshire SG12 9ET

ISBN 1–85326–814–3

*Previous page: the 1970 Mercedes-Benz Type C III
had a four rotor Wankel engine which produced a
top speed in excess of 300km/h (200 mph)*

Right: the unmistakable Ferrari F40

Designed and produced by Superlaunch Ltd
P O Box 207, Abingdon, Oxfordshire OX13 6TA, England
Text conversion and pagination by
August Filmsetting, St Helens, England
Colour separation by Seagull Reproductions Ltd, London
Printed and bound in the Czech Republic by Svoboda

FOREWORD

Classic Sports Cars is a survey of postwar sports cars from around the world, arranged alphabetically by manufacturer. It is worth pointing out, however, that the definition of a sports car found in a dictionary will not be accurately given to everyone's satisfaction, and thus I have tried to comply with the manufacturers' classifications. Comments to this end have generally been made in the individual entries.

Note: owing to space restrictions, coverage of companies which offered kit cars, and of those manufacturers which made copies of original classics; even if some of them may have proved better than the originals, has been severely curtailed or entirely omitted

Abarth Italy

Building its own competition cars since 1955, Abarth began with the Tipo 207 Spyder, which comprised modified Fiat 1100 running gear and an open two seat body. Separately from Fiat, Abarth made by arrangement with Porsche, the Porsche-Abarth Carrera GTL of 1960, with a Porsche 356B chassis. Abarth also had an arrangement with Simca until 1965, when Chrysler took over the latter company. Abarth always retained its close relationship with Fiat, and when in financial trouble in 1971, Fiat took over the company and made it its rallying division.

Above: *1994 AC Cobra*

Left: *1962 Porsche Abarth*

AC UK

Founded in 1908, it marketed its successful Ace after the Second World War, and just when things were getting desperate, Carroll Shelby came to the rescue by fitting a 4 litre Ford

4

Below: *the reborn Alfa Romeo Spyder*

engine into the Ace chassis, to create the AC Cobra. AC was sold in 1984. Today the AC Cobra is hand built at the rate of 40 per year with the AC Ace. Bodies are aluminium, and the Cobra, like the Ace, has a 225bhp Ford 5 litre V8 engine.

Acura Japan
This is the name used for marketing some Honda models in the USA, including the NS-X of 1990.

Alfa Romeo Italy
The outstanding marque of the interwar period, Alfa has concentrated on volume car production since the Second World War. Between 1946 and 1951, the prewar Tipo 158 racers won every race for which they were entered. In 1987, Alfa-Romeo was taken over by Fiat.

Notable sports cars since the Second World War include the 2500SS (Super Sport) of 1947–52, followed by the 1900 Super Sprint (1954–8), the Guilietta Sprint Veloce, and open top version the Guilietta Spyder and the Guilietta SS and S2, with bodies designed by Bertone and Zagato respectively.

In 1963 came the Guilia T2, followed by the TZ2, capable of a top speed of 240km/h (150mph). The Duetto appeared in 1966, with body design by Pininfarina, which in various guises has remained in production until today. The 1750 Spyder Veloce made its appearance in 1967 and was succeeded by the 2000 in 1970.

Alpine France

Société Automobiles Alpine was founded in 1955 by rally driver Jean Redélé, and its first car was based on the Renault 4cv floor plan and named the A106 Mille Miles.

The classic Alpine shape was established in 1963, with the launch of the A110, based on the Renault R8 engine; this came first, second and third in the 1969 Alpine Rally. A total 8,200 of the type were produced, and were sold through the Renault agencies.

Renault finally took over the company in 1974; four years later, a Renault Alpine A442 was to win the Le Mans 24 Hour race. The GTA 2+2 fibreglass coupé was launched in 1985, with the 'Le Mans' limited version next for 1990, complete with body bulges and wider wheels. A turbocharged engine produced 185bhp capable of 235km/h (146mph) and 0–97km/h (0–60mph) in 6.8 seconds.

Alvis UK

One of the great names in sports car production, Alvis was star-

Above: *an Alpine A110 which remained in production until 1977*

Below: *the unsuccessful Alvis TB14 was powered by an 1,892cc engine*

ted in 1919 and had its heyday in the 1930s. After the Second World War investment was meagre, and the company slid out of production in 1966, a year after having been purchased by Rover.

The TB14 entered production in 1949, just 100 being built before the TB21 made its appearance.

AMC USA

Hudson and Nash amalgamated in 1954 to form the American Motors Corporation, which had climbed to be the fourth largest of the North American car makers within five years, with an annual production exceeding 400,000 units. Production of a fastback coupé, the Javelin, was begun in 1968; the two seat version of this was known as the AMX, which appeared in a wide variety of engine options.

Aston Martin UK

Production was started in 1922, and the company sold to David Brown in 1947. Racing success followed in 1959, with a win at Le Mans and the World Sports Car Championship. In 1972, the company was sold to Company Developments Limited, and was sold again in 1975. In 1980, it changed hands yet again, with control passing into new ownership in 1983 before being sold in 1987 to Ford.

Production after the Second World War saw the introduction of the DB1 in 1948, fitted with a 2 litre engine producing 90bhp. The DB1, of which only 15 were produced, gave way to the DB2 in 1950 which was powered by the 105bhp Lagonda engine. A DB2 came fifth at Le Mans in 1950 and triumphed with a 1,2,3 in class in the Tourist Trophy.

Below: *the AMX had as standard a 4,752cc 225bhp V8 engine*

The following year a third place was achieved at Le Mans with a lightweight version. In both 1952 and 1953 they won their class in the *Mille Miglia*.

The DB4, which appeared in 1958, was the first entirely new car to be produced under David Brown's ownership. Powered by a 3.7 litre straight six, which delivered 240bhp, it also had a new four speed gear box. The top speed was 226km/h (141mph), with 0–97km/h (0–60mph) in 8.5 seconds. The DB4 also appeared as the DB4GT (Vantage) and the classic 1961 DB4GT Zagato.

The DB4 gave way to the DB5 in 1963, which in turn was replaced by the DB6 in 1965, of which 1,753 had been produced by the time the run ended in

Overleaf, top: *1957 Aston Martin DB2/4 Mk III two door*
Overleaf, bottom: *1965 DB5 sports convertible*

Previous page, top: *1966 Aston Martin DB6 Vantage*

Previous page, bottom: *1994 DB7*

1970. By this time the DBS was also in production, with a new body styled by William Towns. The DBS V8 model entered production in 1969, with a 5.3 litre dohc V8 engine which from 1972 was known as the V8 Vantage.

The Volante entered production in 1978, and the Volante Vantage in 1986. The new style Virage became available in 1989, with styling by John Heffernan and Ken Greenley, and a top speed of 252km/h (157mph).

Austin UK

This once great manufacturer was founded in 1905, and made its mark with the Austin Seven in 1922. The company was merged with Morris in 1952, to form British Motor Corporation (BMC), then Britain's largest motor manufacturer. Sports car production ended in the 1960s and the name finally disappeared in the 1980s.

After the Second World War, the first sports model to be produced was the A40 Sports, with a Jensen built body and a 50bhp twin carb four cylinder 1,200cc engine.

Austin-Healey UK

Founded as the Donald Healey Motor Company, it had produced a limited number of sports cars when, in 1952, a two seater model was built from Austin components. The car was tested in Belgium where it recorded 188km/h (117mph) and was later to star at the Earls Court Motor Show, where Sir Leonard Lord, MD of BMC, promptly bought the company.

The very beautiful looking Austin-Healey 100 appeared in 1953, with a 2.6 litre four cylinder Austin 90 engine capable of reaching a top speed of 165km/h (103mph) and 0–97km/h (0–60mph) in 10.3 seconds. Coil springs were used, double wishbone front suspension and semi-elliptical sprung live rear axle. The 100s entered limited production the following year, intended for racing; they had front and rear disc brakes.

A new model number, the 100/6, appeared in 1956 with some styling changes which included an elliptical radiator grille and a bonnet scoop. The tiny Austin-Healey 'Frog-eye' Sprite appeared in 1958, having a lot of parts commonality with the Austin A35. Not particularly fast, with a top speed of 130km/h (80mph), it was nevertheless a much loved and popular priced car, of which

Above: *1955 Austin-Healey 100/4 BNI*

nearly 50,000 units were built between 1958 and 1961.

The Sprite II followed in 1961, without frog eyes, and the restyling was more conventional. Disc brakes were fitted to the front and by 1962 the engine size had increased to 1,098cc, producing 56bhp and capable of a top speed of 136km/h (85mph). Options included detachable hard tops. The Mk III appeared in 1964, the Mk IV in 1966. The Austin Sprite, of which just over 1,000 were produced, existed solely because at the end of production the agreement between Austin and Healey had ended.

Auto Union Germany

The result of a merger in 1932 between Audi, DKW, Horch and Wanderer, the marque made its name with a series of 1930s *Grand Prix* cars. The company, being in eastern Germany, was nationalised after the War, when cars were marketed as IFA models. In 1950, two ex-DKW executives restarted production in West Germany, with a model based on the Auto Union 1000. Production began in 1958, but in 1965 the Audi name was revived and DKW dropped. In 1958, a sports two seater, the 1000SP, was launched, which stayed in production until 1965; power was provided by a 980cc 55bhp three cylinder two stroke.

b + b Germany
Rainer Buchmann's styling studio has specialised in customising cars since the early 1970s. During the late 1970s, it built the CW311 gull wing mid-engined coupé powered by a Mercedes-Benz V8 engine. The top speed was claimed to be 320km/h (200mph) and 0–97km/h (0–60mph) took 4.5 seconds.

b + b styled Porsche 928 cabriolet at the German Motor Show, 1981

Bitter Germany
With unofficial help from Opel, which did not want to market an Erich Bitter car under its own name, Bitter was enabled to market the car under his own. The car, based on the Chevrolet engined Opel Diplomat floor plan, became the Bitter CD, a 2+2 fastback coupé.

Baur built the bodies at the rate of three per week, front suspension was by coil springs and double wishbones, and the de Dion rear axle was suspended on coil springs. Disc brakes were fitted to all four wheels. The Chevrolet V8 engine produced a top speed of 210km/h (130mph) from its 5,345cc 230bhp.

In 1979, the original CD model was replaced by the SC, based on the Opel Senator floor plan and powered by a 180bhp 3 litre straight six engine. Variants included a 3.9 litre engined version in 1983, and a convertible in 1984.

Following a break in production because of financial problems, Bitter was back in the market in 1987 with the Type III, a two seat sports car based on the Opel Omega floor plan and which was made available in both coupé and convertible forms; MacPherson struts were employed on the front suspension and on the rear coil springs and trailing arms. All round disc brakes with ABS were fitted, and the engine was a 3 litre straight six capable of a speed of 227km/h (141mph). Bodies were now being built by Maggiora in Torino, and finished by Steyr Puch in Austria.

BMW Germany
The builder of aero engines and motorcycles turned to car production in 1929, producing the Austin Seven under licence. In 1934, it produced its own design and in 1936 launched the 328, a leading sports car of the period. In the period after the Second World War, BMW developed its successful series of small saloons. By the 1970s, BMW cars were much in demand with their saloons also scoring on the racetracks. It pioneered turbocharging in Europe, with the 2002 Turbo in 1973.

The Model 507 was launched in 1950, and remained in production for three years, over which period just 253 units were produced. BMW's first postwar two seater was available with both

Above: *BMW's M1 was in production between 1978–80*

Below: *a 1990 model Z1, which had a top speed of 218km/h (136mph) and could reach 97km/h (60mph) from a standing start in 7.9 seconds. One interesting feature is that the doors slid down into the shell for access*

a rag top or in a coupé version with a 150bhp engine. The 507 was capable of a top speed of 200km/h (124mph) and 0–97km/h (0–60mph) in 8.8 seconds. Later production cars had front discs fitted.

It was 1979 before BMW was back in production with a sports car; however, the M1 was never produced in large enough quantities for it to be homologated in the right race category. Its racing history is therefore not exciting, but as a street car it was a far different proposition, powered by BMW's 3.5 litre straight six 277bhp dohc four valve per cylinder engine, which was mid-mounted in a space frame with independent suspension all round by coil springs and double wishbones. The top speed was 360km/h (162mph), and 0–97km/h (0–60mph) was achieved in 5.5 seconds.

Between 1986 and 1991, BMW produced the Z1, originally built as a concept car with a monocoque of steel and carbon composition, BMW's 'Z-axle' wishbone rear suspension and MacPherson strut front suspension. Production was ended in 1991, after a production run of 8,000 units.

Although not considered a sports car by the manufacturer, it is hard to ignore BMW's cur-rent 8 series, bristling with technology and powered by the V12 engine; the 850i has per-formance to match its style.

Bricklin USA/Canada
A lot of parallels can be drawn between Malcolm Bricklin and John Delorean, in that both were successful American automobile salesmen, both conceived a 'safety' sports car with good lines and gull wing doors plus a rot resistant body, both sold their concepts to a foreign government (in the case of Bricklin, this was New Brunswick, Canada, which fin-anced the production in order to bring work to a depressed area).

There are more similarities: neither New Brunswick (or, in Delorean's case, Northern Ireland), had any car produc-tion experience, both concepts were well received at promo-tional car shows and good order books were built up, but as the cars rolled off the production line, they proved virtually un-saleable. Numerous faults added to the ever rising product costs, and as the retail price in-creased production slumped, and the government refused to provide new money to throw after the losses already incur-red; in New Brunswick's case, $23 million.

The factory was closed and the Bricklin SV–1 consigned to automobile history, along with that other infamous headline maker, the Delorean DMC-Z. Some 780 SV–1s were produced in 1974, together with a further 2,117 the following year, prior to the company entering receivership in September.

The 1974 production featured electrically operated gull wing doors, which should the battery fail would trap the driver inside, and a fibreglass body which was prone to cracking; mechanically it had front disc brakes and a 5.9 litre American Motors V8 engine which delivered 220bhp and a top speed of 195km/h (122mph). The later model used both engines and transmissions from Ford, with the 5,752cc V8 slightly less impressive with a top speed of 190km/h (118mph).

Bristol UK
Originating from the Bristol Aircraft Company after the Second World War, it took possession of some BMW designs as part of the War reparations. In 1960, the car and aircraft factions of the business split, with the car company becoming a private concern owned by Sir George White with Tony Crook a director since 1966.

The first postwar model, the 400, launched in 1947, was very much a BMW 326 derivative, with 327-based aluminium body and 328-based six cylinder 1,971cc cross pushrod engine;

1950 Bristol 401, of which just 650 were built

15

the top speed was claimed as being 151km/h (94mph).

The 401 appeared in 1948, a much roomier car, and intended originally for export only, along with the 402 cabriolet. In 1953, the 403 was launched, still basically a 401, the engine producing a modest 100bhp. A two seater version was also available, the 404. The 405 of 1954 had four doors, although a two door cabriolet version (of which just 43 were built) was made.

The 406 Zagato was the last Bristol to use a BMW-based engine, and since then Bristol has continued with its traditional chassis, which has been continuously developed up to the current Britannia Brigand Turbo, which still relies on the Chrysler V8, a line that began in 1962.

Bugatti France

The legend of Ettore Bugatti is such that this famous marque has recently been revived again, but Ettore died in 1947 and there was no natural continuation of car production, despite a brief revival in 1951 by Roland Bugatti. The brief effort in 1951 actually lasted until 1956, although only six units were produced in the period. The T101 was even then little more than a modified 1930s Type 57. It featured solid front and rear axles, with suspension by semi-elliptical springs. After a long absence, Bugatti is back for the 1990s with the EB 110 GT, a beautiful mid-engined four wheel drive supercar.

The EB 110 GT, top speed 346 km/h (213mph)

16

Buick USA

The company was founded in 1903, and a founder member in 1908 of General Motors. The Buick range has always been the conservative marque, but broke with tradition in 1988, when it launched the Reatta, a two seater coupé based on the floor plan of the Riviera saloon. Power was supplied by a 3.8 litre V6 engine, mounted transversely. Top speed was assessed as 200km/h (124mph). A convertible was offered from 1990.

Cadillac USA

Founded in the same year as Buick, it also joined General Motors in 1908, becoming the conglomerate's luxury marque. After the Second World War Cadillac led the 'fins and chrome' fad. In 1986, the Allante was launched, a luxury two seater with body styling by Pininfarina. In 1988, the engine size

Caterham JPA 1990s style

was increased to a 4.5 litre fuel injected V8 which was mounted transversely at the front, and delivered 200bhp. The top speed was 200km/h (124mph) and 0–97km/h (0–60mph) took 8.9 seconds.

Caterham UK

After Lotus ceased building the legendary Chapman-designed Seven, Caterham Cars set up production under licence and since 1973 has been the only authorised maker of the Lotus Seven. It began with the series Four model, but revived the series Three in 1974. Harsh, draughty and thrilling to drive, today the Super Seven is available in five models from the 1.4 litre four cylinder in line 103bhp Rover twin cam engine to the 2 litre 175bhp Vauxhall twin cam engine.

Chevrolet USA

Taking its name from racing driver Louis Chevrolet in 1911, and becoming one of the most popular makes in North America, the company offered good value for money. In 1917 Chevrolet became GM's low priced marque and reached third spot in US sales by 1920 and best seller in 1931, ahead of Ford, reaching its 15 millionth sale in 1939. In 1951, GM's head of styling, Harley Earl, suggested the production of a low priced 150bhp sports car, and the result was the launch in 1953 of the Corvette.

The original 1953/4 'Vette which sold just under 4,000 units had a lot of teething troubles, to the point that it almost never saw the light of day. Even in production, 315 in 1953, the door seals on the fibreglass body caused problems for the first production batch.

The 1955 model was a better product, and was powered by Ed Cole's new 4.3 litre V8 engine with a three speed manual gear box as an option. The new engine produced 195bhp and the top speed was upped to 191km/h (119mph) with an acceleration that took it from 0–97km/h (0–60mph) in 8.7 seconds.

For the following year, the body was restyled and the power increased to provide the 1956 model with a top speed of 210km/h (130mph). Production between 1956–7 totalled just under 10,000 but between 1958–60 a further 29,000 were produced. These were slower than 1957–8's Corvette, although one did just manage to finish eighth in the 1960 24 hour Le Mans endurance race.

The 'Vette body was restyled for 1961, and in 1962 a new 360bhp engine option pushed the car from 0–97km/h (0–60mph) in a brief 5.5 seconds.

The Sting Ray was launched in 1963, with a shorter wheelbase than the Corvette. It was also a completely differently styled car, available as either a coupé or a roadster. Production lasted until 1967, when it was to be replaced by the Corvette Stingray, although it was not called a Stingray until 1969. The chassis style was the same as the original Sting Ray, but 177.8mm (7 inches) longer on the same wheelbase because the 'impact' bumpers were incorporated in the design of the body.

The option range continued to be expanded. The Corvette of 1978 had a smoother fastback body and dropped the Stingray name. The base engine was now a 5.7 litre V8 which produced 185bhp. It was not until 1984 that the next all new Corvette

Above: *the Corvette Stingray of 1975 came from a production run of nearly 340,000*

Below: *Corvette convertible of 1990*

appeared with a pressed steel back bone chassis. It was originally offered as a 'Targa top', the roadster making its appearance in 1986, and the option range included a Callaway Twin Turbo version, which offered a top speed on the coupé version of 300km/h (187mph) and 0–97km/h (0–60mph) in 4.6 seconds.

The last Corvette to arrive was the ZR–1 in 1989, with a Lotus-developed dohc four valves per cylinder 5.7 litre V8 which delivered 380bhp through a six speed ZF gear box. The top speed is in the 275km/h (172mph) range, the new body shape is two inches wider and the tail is more rounded in the 1990s style.

Although the Corvette was Chevrolet's sports car, Chevrolet also produced the Camaro from 1967, a muscle car that was sold under the Pontiac badge, and the Beretta 2+2 coupé from 1987, a sporting compact with front wheel drive.

Chrysler USA
The Chrysler Corporation was formed in 1925, and originally sold mid-range popular cars, although it did manage to come in as third and fourth places in their class in the 1928 Le Mans. After the Second World War, Chrysler became a multinational in 1958 by buying a

part of Simca, which has been wholly owned since 1963, and added the Rootes Group in 1959 and 15% of Mitsubishi in 1970.

However, the giant corporation experienced problems in the late 1970s, which had worsened a decade later. The Corporation's sports cars were mainly those of Lamborghini and Dodge, but in 1983 Chrysler launched its first two seater, the GS coupé, also sold as the Dodge Daytona, with a Shelby top of the range version with a five speed manual gear box and a 174bhp turbocharged four cylinder 2,213cc engine capable of a 222km/h (138mph) top speed. The Chrysler TC by Maserati was introduced in 1987.

Cisitalia Italy
The company was created in 1939, but the first car was not offered until 1946, a single seater racing car with an 1,100cc Fiat engine. There followed then a two seat lightweight competition car in either coupé or open variant. Later in 1947 the first Cisitalia road cars were produced initially in Italy, but when the founder Piero Dusio ran into financial problems in 1949, he moved the company to Argentina, where production continued.

The 202 Gran Sport was based on the Fiat 1100, with the

The 1947 Cisitalia Coupé Pininfarina

1,089cc four cylinder engine and four speed gear box. However, the body was styled by Pininfarina. Dusio's son then tried to rebuild the company in Italy, but his sports coupé version of the Fiat 1900 was not a success, and despite other attempts, the company finally closed in 1965.

Citroën France
Citroën began making cars in 1919, and made its mark with the classic Traction Avant of 1934. The company was acquired by the Michelin tyre company in the 1930s, and although not known for the production of sports cars, launched the SM in 1970. The production of the Maserati-

engined car ceased in 1975, soon after Peugeot-Talbot took over the company after almost 13,000 had been made. The body featured six headlamps, of which four swivelled with the steering wheel. The top speed of the 170bhp 2.7 litre dohc V6 was 225km/h (140mph).

Daimler UK
Britain's first motor manufacturer Daimler was initially set up in 1893 to market Gottleib Daimler's patents. From 1900 to 1950, Daimler was the first choice of the British Royal Family. After the Second World War, Daimler was forced to move down market, and produced a series of 2.5 litre saloons. In 1960, the company was taken over by Jaguar.

The Conquest Century Roadster was first introduced in 1954, powered by a straight six 2,433cc engine which gave 100bhp though only a top speed of 143km/h (89mph). Production covered only 65 units, and it was replaced by the Conquest Century Sports Coupé in 1956. This had better braking and a third seat was added, but production was still only 54 examples.

The more popular SP250 appeared in 1959, powered by a 2,548cc 'over square' V8 engine, which developed 140bhp and managed a top speed of 200km/h (124mph) and made 0–97km/h (0–60mph) in 8.8 seconds. The SP250 had all round disc brakes and room for two children in the rear.

DB France
Charles Deutsch and René Bonnet began their association in 1939 with two Citroën-based specials, which remained virtually untried until 1945, when they were both entered for the first race meeting in Paris after the Second World War. There then followed a more advanced car, based on the Citroën 2cv engine, which produced 75bhp.

Further single seat Citroën-based cars followed, together with sports car versions, until Deutsch and Bonnet formed Automobiles DB in 1949, building a 500cc Panhard-based car

for Formula 3 in 1950. Their sports versions followed; by the mid–1950s 750cc DB Panhards were beginning to dominate their race class with wins at Le Mans, Sebring, the *Mille Miglia* and in 1954 the Tourist Trophy.

In 1952, DB launched a coupé based on Panhard Dyna suspension and from 1955 the aluminium bodies were replaced with fibreglass shells and engine options were extended to 1,000 and 1,300cc. The partnership ended in 1961, when Bonnet wanted to extend his relationship with Renault while Deutsch was determined to remain with Panhard.

Delage France
One of the great marques, the company was formed at the start of this century, though its first breakthrough did not come until the 1920s. In 1935 it was acquired by Delahaye, and after the Second World War it merged with Hotchkiss, but this was to little avail. By the following year, 1954, the new group had failed. Its initial postwar offering had been an upgraded version of the 1937 D6, which had a short stroke 3 litre engine.

Delahaye France
Delahaye was founded as a brick making factory in 1845,

moving slowly towards the production of steam, then gas, engines. In 1894 it built its first car, and by the 1930s, following the absorbtion of Delage, was making upmarket high performance cars. Successes at Le Mans before the Second World War included a second place in 1937 and a first, second and fourth the following year. Postwar decline was rapid, with sports car production, which had been ten cars per week, falling to a total of three for the whole of 1953.

The T135 model spanned the war years, entering production in 1936 and winning both the Monte Carlo Rally and the Marseilles *Grand Prix* prewar. After the War, a new 3.6 litre straight six engine was fitted, with an electrically operated eight speed gear box. Production ended in 1951. The T175 of 1948–51 was followed by the final model, the T235, of which less than 100 were made between 1951 and 1953.

Delorean USA/UK

The result of official efforts to help create jobs in Northern Ireland, the company was heavily reliant on uncritical financial backing from the British Government. The car itself was the brainchild of John Z Delorean, and promoted as an exclusive sports car although in order to make financial sense it would have had to have outsold every other car in its category. In effect, the car, the DMC–2, was a gimmick car full of extras.

Between 1981 and 1982, production totalled 8,583 although it is not sure where these went to or if they were all completed. The layout was based on the Lotus Élan, with Lotus developing the independently sprung backbone chassis. The body was styled by Giugiaro, and the car powered by a 2.8 litre Renault V6 engine. The manufacture and finish of the cars was a disgrace, the numerous problems encountered by the purchasers too many to list, and the project folded.

De Tomaso Italy

Argentinian racing driver Alejandro de Tomaso had established his company in the heartland of Italian sports car production, at Módena. There, in addition to production of his own De Tomaso marque, he acquired other prestige marques including Maserati and Innocenti, the styling houses of Vignale and Ghia (controlled via his brother in law), and the motorcycle makers Benelli and Moto Guzzi.

Left: *the ill-fated Delorean*

The De Tomaso Vallelungo
was launched in 1965, his first
road car; it was planned as an
open two seater with a pressed
steel backbone chassis and all
independent suspension by coil
springs and double wishbones.
The car was powered by a 1.5
litre Ford Cortina engine. A
mid-engined coupé version was
actually produced, but soon
dropped.

In 1967, the Mangusta used
the Vallelunga chassis adjusted
to accommodate a Ford 4.7 litre
V8, which delivered 306bhp with
a top speed of 250km/h (155mph).
This was a brittle beast, but
looked superb and production
reached 400 before the model
was replaced in 1971, by the
Pantera. The mid-engined Pantera has been the mainstay of
De Tomaso production, re-
maining in production until the
present.

Power was originally provided by a 5,763cc Ford V8, and
production was progressing
well with US sales handled by
Ford through its Lincoln-
Mercury network; however, the
car always gave problems, and
in 1974 Ford took the opportun-

Left: *the current De Tomaso mid-
engined Pantera, capable of a top
speed of 240km/h (149mph)*

ity of the fuel crisis to break
the agreement. As part of the
severance, Ford took over
Ghia.

In 1990, de Tomaso sold Maserati to Fiat and revised the
styling of the Pantera. The 1994
Pantera 200 has been restyled
again, this time by Ghia, and
the complete revamp has produced a much more acceptable
result, with increased head-
room and legroom, and a body
which now includes Kevlar
panels.

DKW Germany
DKW launched its first car in
1928, and went on to become one
of the founding partners of
Auto Union. After the Second
World War, the company was
nationalised by the East German Government, but in 1949
the name was revived in West
Germany and a series of front
wheel drive cars were produced
with three cylinder, two stroke
900cc engines. Between 1957 and
1958, a number of small two seat
fibreglass coupés were produced
under the model name of
Monza, with a slightly more
powerful 55bhp 980cc engine,
which provided a top speed of
160km/h (100mph).

Dodge USA
The Dodge brothers made their
first car in 1914, which quickly

became the second most popular American marque. Dodge joined the Chrysler Corporation in 1928, and after the Second World War there was a long wait for a Dodge sports car.

The Charger, which appeared in 1968, had the right image but Dodge finally broke through with the 1990 Stealth sports coupé, a Mitsubishi 3000 GT look alike. Dodge had been selling Mitsubishi models in North America since 1970.

The base Stealth has a 12V 3 litre V6 and is now sold alongside the 1992 Dodge Daytona IROC R/T model, with a 2.2 litre dohc turbocharged and intercooled engine. These have been joined in the showroom by the Dodge Viper, a limited production wind in your face roadster equipped with an 8 litre V10 producing 294kW (400PS) at 5,500rpm through a six speed gear box with a maximum speed of 233km/h (145mph).

Below: *1985 Dodge Shelby Charger*

Above: *the Elva Courier Mk IV coupé, which was built in small quantities by Trojan*

Elva UK
Frank Nichols' first Mike Chapman-built car was the CSM, which gave way to an improved version christened Elva. It was designed by 'Mac' Witts, and met with some success in North America in SCCA racing.

In 1958 the Courier was launched, with a fibreglass body, tubular frame, coil spring and double wishbone front suspension and a live rear axle with coil springs and radius arms. The engines ranged from 1,489 to 1,798cc, and were from the MGA or MGB. Production lasted until 1961, when it was replaced by the Mk III. Coupé versions were offered and by 1968 the Ford Cortina GT engine was an option.

The lovely Elva GT 160 was launched in 1963, but failed to get off the ground; three prototypes were produced, with a GT body styled by Trevor Fiore and built in Italy by Fissore. The engine was a BMW 2 litre.

Facel Vega France

Founded in 1938, Forges et Ateliers de Construction d'Eure et de Loire SA made machine tools for the aircraft industry, and only began making car bodies after the Second World War. In 1954, it launched its Vega, powered by a 4.5 litre De Soto V8 engine which produced 180bhp. Later versions, including the FVS, were powered by a 5.4 litre Chrysler V8 and could achieve a top speed of 210km/h (130mph). In 1959 an upgraded Vega, the HK500, was introduced with an even bigger 6.3 litre 360bhp engine. A further upgrading was to produce the Facel II in 1962, the same year in which the company went into receivership.

From 1960, the Facellia was launched, a smaller two seat car which was available as a hard top coupé or a convertible with a 1,647cc dohc four cylinder engine. Finally, between 1963 and 1964, a 1,780cc engined model, the Facel III, appeared and sold well, but not in such quantity as to save the company from bankruptcy in 1965.

Ferrari Italy

Enzo Anselmo Ferrari was a true titan, who used a life spanning 90 years to vent his ambition and passion in founding the company to build the cars which bear his name. The raw power, combined with the sophistication and style which became the hallmark of his cars, are emblematic of the man's personality.

Attaining this goal was not easy. Enzo was no scholar, openly admitting that he had 'a deep rooted aversion to study'. At the age of ten, his imagination had been stirred when his father took him to watch a road race, north of Bologna. Soon after, he decided to become a racing driver, and by the time he was 14, he was contributing sports reports to a local newspaper. Three years on, he was drafted into the army.

Appropriately enough, as *ferraro* means 'blacksmith' in Italian, Enzo was assigned to the mountain artillery, shoeing mules. The following year, first his father died of pneumonia, and shortly afterwards his elder brother also died of a mysterious illness contracted during his military service. Enzo too fell seriously ill, but survived to be discharged at the end of the war.

Although his colonel had provided a letter of introduction to the huge Fiat automotive manufacturer in Torino, Enzo endured a period of acute poverty and near destitution

Top: *1957 GT*

Centre: *1965 275 GTS*

Bottom: *1971 365 GTB*

before finding work for an entrepreneur as a test and delivery driver in the same area. This business was based on stripping the bodies from surplus military trucks to be sold as bare chassis to a company in Milano, which refitted them with sporty coachwork.

From this mundane beginning, Enzo went on to become a successful racing driver for Alfa Romeo, running his own Scuderia team for nine years before leaving in 1939 to set up Auto-Avio Costruzioni di Ferrari in September of that year, with his first car, the Type 815, running in the *Mille Miglia* on 28 April 1940.

The Tipo 125, with a 1.5 litre engine, appeared ahead of the 2 litre Tipo 166 in 1947. Both had sohc V12 engines and five speed gear boxes, and the 150bhp 166 powered its way to early racing success with wins at Le Mans and in the *Mille Miglia*. When the 195 appeared in 1950, the engine was enlarged to 2,341cc but the same chassis was kept. Only 25 units were built and the model was not a racing success, but the 212 with a longer wheelbase and a 2,562cc engine was.

At the same time, Ferrari went into production with the America series: 340, 342, and 375. In 1953, 195 production ended and was replaced by the 250 series; Export, Europa and GT. The GT marked the point at which the relationship between Enzo Ferrari and Battista 'Pinin' Farina began to bloom, and Ferrari SpA became a volume producer with over 900 250 GT units being built each with Colombo's classic 2,953cc engine.

The 375 America was replaced in 1956 by the 410 Superamerica, with a 340bhp 5 litre engine capable of reaching a top speed of 217km/h (135mph). From 1958, the power was increased to 360bhp and the top speed pushed up to 250km/h (155mph). Ferrari introduced disc brakes on the 250 GT SWB of 1959. The wheelbase had been shortened to 2.4m (94.5in) and the result was stunning.

Top: *1979 GTS*

Centre: *the 1982 400i was the last version of this model*

Bottom: *1986 288 GTO*

A luxury version, the 250 Lusso, was produced from 1962. The 250 GT 2+2 entered production in 1960, the same year as the 400 Superamerica, and in 1962 came the GTO, which was a 250 Testarossa with a roof; it also had a 300bhp engine. In two years, just 39 of these 250 GTOs were produced, but they are beautiful and today very much a collector's trophy.

Production of the GTO was replaced by the 250 Le Mans, which was the first mid-engined Ferrari GT with power supplied by a 320bhp V12, which gave the

car the first and second places at Le Mans in 1965. At the same time, the 275 GTB (Berlinetta), with a 3.3 litre engine, was being produced alongside a GTS (Spyder), both with all independent suspension and five speed gear boxes. The GTB coupé was rated at 280bhp against the 260bhp rated GTS convertible.

In 1964, the Superfast 500 made its *début*, with a 400bhp 5 litre engine and body styling by Pininfarina. The 330 GTC/GTS and the 365 California both appeared in 1966, the luxury California with a 4.4 litre 'quad cam' and another Pininfarina body; but the following year, the even more luxurious 365 GT 2+2 appeared and took over as Ferrari's most luxurious and largest model. It had a 2.641m (104in) wheelbase and an sohc 4.4 litre V12 engine which produced 320bhp. There were also 356 GTC and GTS versions available from 1968.

When the famous Dino 206 GT first appeared in 1967, it was without a Ferrari badge. The engine named after Enzo's son, a small capacity V6 mounted transversely amidships, was built by Fiat. The car was not a success, unlike the Pininfarina styled 365 GTB Daytona, which appeared in 1968. An immediate success, this combined

the 275 chassis with the 4.4 litre 'quad cam' engine, which produced a roaring 275km/h (170mph).

The Dino 246 GT was better in 1969; the engine size was upped to 2.4 from 2 litres and, although it was the cheapest Ferrari ever built, sales were 2,800 units, together with a further 1,000+ of the GTS (Spyder) version, which appeared in 1972.

The 365 GT was replaced in 1971 by the 365 GTC/4 2+2, that was also front engined, but was short lived and was in turn replaced the following year by the 365 GT4, with a longer wheelbase. The model was upgraded in 1976, as the 400i with a 4.8 litre fuel injected engine which produced 340bhp.

The first Dino with a Ferrari badge was the 308 GT4 of 1973, styled this time by Bertone. It was powered by a 3 litre dohc V8 engine, and was quicker at 240km/h (150mph). It was also a real 2+2, but the Dino name was dropped for the 1977 model.

The 5 litre flat 12 Berlinetta Boxer engine with the pistons which move away from each other first appeared in the 1976 model 512 BB. This was an update of the 365 GT4BB, which had introduced the boxer engine with the mid-mounted dohc 4.4 litre in 1973. Fuel injection was available from the early 1980s, and a few Targa-top versions were also made.

Although the Dino name was now dropped, its successor was the 1975 308 GTB, with a shorter wheelbase and a 2,921cc dry sump engine. It heralded a new era for Ferrari, with fibreglass body panels and a Pininfarina body style that was to be the benchmark for future Ferrari models. The 308 and 208 GTB and GTS models remained in production until 1981, by which time the Mondial 8 had made a

Above: *the 328*
Below: *the 456GT*

sensational appearance.

The Mondial shared the chassis of the Dino GT4, which it replaced, but the longer wheelbase produced space for a proper four seater. The engine was a 3 litre V8 with fuel injection which produced 214bhp and 230km/h (143mph). In 1982 a 240bhp *quattrovalvole* engine was offered as an option, and in 1985 the standard engine was upgraded to a 260bhp 3.2 litre. From 1983, a cabriolet version was also offered.

Production was switched from the 308 GTB in 1981 to the 308i, with a less powerful fuel injection engine. By 1982, this had also received the *quattrovalvole* engine, which improved performance; the engine of its sister model, the 208 GT, was turbocharged.

The 308 received a further lease of life in 1985, when the 3.2 litre engine then used in the Mondial was also introduced to the 308 and helped to make the model Ferrari's best seller of all time. In 1984, Ferrari launched a planned production run of 200 of the GTO, so that homologation could be achieved for Group B competition. The GTO resembled the 308 GTB in looks, and also used the same 3 litre V8 engine. In the GTO, however, it was not mounted horizontally but vertically in a 111.76mm (4.4in) longer wheelbase, with twin turbochargers added together with Weber-Marelli electronic fuel injection. The GTO produced 400bhp and had a top speed of 305km/h (190mph) and acceleration of 0–97km/h (0–60mph) in 5 seconds.

In 1984 the aluminium bodied Pininfarina styled Testarossa was introduced to replace the Berlinetta Boxer. Four years later, Ferrari celebrated its 40th birthday with the F40,

powered by a variation of the 3 litre *quattrovalvole* V8 with twin IHI turbochargers. It produced 471bhp and a top speed of a cool 325km/h (201mph) with 0–97km/h (0–60mph) achieved in less than 4 seconds – quite a party piece.

The following year saw the introduction of the 348 tb coupé and Targa and the Mondial t coupé and convertible. The 348 tb had radiators mounted in the sides, making it wider than previous models, and in addition a

longitudinally mounted engine. The underbody allowed for the control panels and steering wheel to be directly ahead of the driver.

The Mondial t was a big improvement in space and luxury, but was not as exciting and was never really a big hit, unlike the stunning new 456 GT 2+2 launched at the 1993 London Motor Show. This was a

Ferrari's first car for the 90s was the 348 tb

completely new Ferrari from its tubular chassis, six speed gear box and 5,473cc V12 engine to its aluminium alloy two door coupé bodywork. The 456 GT claims a top speed of over 308.75km/h (190mph).

Earlier in 1993, the 348 Spyder was launched, an open topped Pininfarina styled supercar powered by the same 3,405cc V8 as the Mondial t. Ferrari's other current model is the 512 TR, just one more of the truly great creations from Módena.

Fiat Italy

Established in 1899, Fiat was quick to distinguish itself in early competitions, which greatly assisted sales of its mid-range mass produced cars. Fiat expanded rapidly in the 1920s, creating SEAT in Spain, Simca in France, and later acquiring among various others Abarth, Alfa Romeo, Autobianchi and Ferrari.

After the Second World War Fiat's additions to the racing car market have not been prolific under its own marque, but it has provided an invaluable contribution of numerous components on a worldwide basis to a large number of small constructors.

The 8V was produced in small numbers between 1952 and 1954, powered by the V8 1,996cc engine, which had pushrods operated by a single camshaft situated at the centre of the V. This was followed by the 1100 Transformabile in 1955, and in 1959 the highly popular 1200 appeared with the 1,100 engine increased to 1,221cc and producing 63bhp, a top speed of 145 km/h (90mph) and capable of 0–97km/h (0–60mph) in 19.1 seconds.

A 1,491cc engined version was also available, designated the 1500S; it had a dohc four cylinder engine which produced 80bhp. Between its introduction in 1965 and 1973, Fiat produced 140,000 850 Spyders, styled by Bertone. The 850 was a four seat coupé with the 843cc engine mounted behind the rear axle line. Reasonably priced and stylish, the performance was not sensational, with a top speed of 140km/h (87mph). Even when the engine size was increased to 903cc in 1968, the top speed was still only 146km/h (91mph).

Another Spyder appeared in 1968, based on the 124 range of models. The 124 Spyder was a 2+2 with double wishbone and coil spring front suspension, and a live rear axle on coil springs located by trailing arms and a Panhard rod. It also had a five speed gear box and disc brakes all round. During the production run, which lasted until 1985 and covered over 125,000 units, a variety of engines were used, all four cylinders with twin overhead camshafts.

The 124 was also developed into an Abarth Rallye version in 1972, with a permanent hard top.

The Ferrari inspired Dino Coupé was launched in 1966, which was prior to Fiat's purchase of Ferrari in 1969. Styled by Bertone, the Dino coupé was a 2+2 also available in a Spyder

Fiat's mass production success came with the mid-engined X1/9

version, which was capable of 205km/h (127mph) and of 0–97km/h (0–60mph) in 8.1 seconds. Sales by Fiat standards were slow, and in an attempt to boost sales the engine was upgraded to 2,418cc. Ironically, by the time the model's production run came to an end, the cars were being built in the Ferrari works at Maranello.

Fiat's last entry into the sports car market was with the X1/9 in 1972, and oddly enough it proved to be the most successful mid-engined mass produced sports car ever. The Targa top was designed by Bertone and the car launched with the 1,290cc four cylinder engine as used in the Fiat 128 saloon, together with the 128 gear box. Production lasted until 1982.

Ford UK
Founded in Manchester in 1911 to assemble US produced Model T components, the company rapidly became the largest European car maker. In 1931, the Dagenham factory was opened and production of the Model Y commenced. It produced engines, especially the 997cc 105E engine, which were used extensively by smaller builders and tuners and were the basis of the Lotus Formula Junior success, but it was not until the 1960s that Ford entered motor sport in a big way and then initially as an attempt to improve its salesroom image.

The GT40 was launched in 1966, specifically aimed at winning the Le Mans 24 Hour race. The car was 1.016m (40in) high and hence the name. Suspension was independent all round by coil springs and double wishbones, the engine was a 4.7 litre

Previous page: *Ford USA Mustang II*

Right: *Ford UK GT Mk III*

dry sump V8 which produced 390bhp through a five speed ZF gear box, and the top speed was 320km/h (200mph), achieved at Le Mans by a works entered car. In total, 107 GT40s were built by Ford Advanced Vehicles' division at Slough.

The Le Mans race was won by a Mk 2 in 1966. The Mk 3 was launched in 1967, but because of policy changes at Ford only seven units were ever produced. In 1970 another sports car, the GT70, was also launched but never went into production, with only four being produced before the project was shelved. It was planned to have been a mid-engined, fibreglass bodied popular sports car.

Ford's last sports car was the 1985 RS200, with a mid-mounted turbocharged 1,803cc Ford Cosworth BDT engine. Drive was to all four wheels via a five speed gear box and the top speed was 225km/h (140mph).

Ford USA
Before the Second World War, Ford had been successful in national races with coupés, but sports cars were never really on the Ford menu. It did react when Chevrolet launched the Corvette, and finally responded in 1955, by means of the Ford Thunderbird, with its 4.8 litre Mercury V8 and top speed of 185km/h (115mph). By 1957, the Thunderbird was an established muscle car, with increased powerplant options.

Ford launched the Mustang GT, an instant success, in 1964 and this is a model name which has persisted. The model went through many changes in the 1970s, to emerge in the 1980s no longer the muscle car of its formative years; today's two door coupé lacks all of the edge that made the golden years of the muscle cars so exciting.

Other current Ford models which might conceivably fit into the sports car category are the elegant Ford Probe LX coupé, which is based on Mazda underpinnings and went on sale in the UK in 1994; and the Taurus SHO, which is powered by a 24 valve 3 litre V6.

Right: *1967 Ford Mustang Tour de France*

Frazer Nash UK

Archie Frazer Nash founded his company in 1924 and after a wobbly start sold out to AFN Ltd in 1926. From the mid–1930s, AFN imported BMWs, which were marketed in the UK as Frazer Nash-BMWs. After the Second World War, the BMW 328 engine formed the basis for the Bristol, in which AFN was a partner. From 1957, until 1986, when Porsche took it over, AFN imported Porsches.

The High Speed was launched in 1948, and after winning at Le Mans the following year, was renamed the Le Mans Replica. Very successful in national competition, one also won the 1951 *Targa Florio*. A lighter weight model followed in 1952, the Le Mans II.

From 1949 the Le Mans Replica had also been offered as a Fast Tourer, which became known as the Mille Miglia and was replaced in production in 1952 by the Targa Florio, in honour of the 1951 victory. This still used the 200 series (Le Mans Mk II) chassis. The first Frazer Nash closed car, the Le Mans Coupé, was launched in 1953 and promptly won its 2 litre class at Le Mans. The Sebring, with the Bristol engine, now tuned to produce 140bhp, was launched in 1954, followed by the Continental GT in 1956, the last Frazer Nash car to be made.

Ginetta UK

Started by the four Walklett brothers in the 1950s, it offered its first product, the G2, as a kit car in 1957. By the 1960s it had progressed to almost fully assembled cars, and managed to keep going after the intro-

duction of VAT to emerge in the 1980s with a new model, the mid-engined G32.

The G3 followed the G2 in 1960, and was somewhat similar but instead of being purely a kit car, the body came almost complete. The G4 was the model that put Ginetta on the road to success, a fibreglass body with coil springs and double wishbone front suspension, live rear axle located by trailing arms and powered by a 997cc Ford 105E engine.

The G5 was launched in 1964, a G4 with a 1,498cc Ford Cortina engine which was later redesignated as the G4 1500. The G4 Series II returned to production in 1981, after a 12 year gap and has sold steadily, mostly in Japan, ever since. The G10 entered production in 1965, with a 4.7 litre Ford V8 engine and a top speed of 240km/h (150mph). The model could not be homologated for SCCA racing in America, so orders collapsed and production stopped. The G11 was a re-engined 910 for the UK market and appeared in 1966, but production was limited.

In 1968, the G15 appeared and proved to be Ginetta's most successful car. It incorporated Triumph Herald front suspension, together with the Hillman Imp engine, transaxle and rear

Ginetta's striking G33

suspension. The top speed was 153km/h (95mph). In 1970 the G21 was launched, a larger version of the G15 with a variety of engine options. The G27 of 1985 was an upgraded G4, and sold mostly in kit form. The G32 was first shown at the NEC Motor Show in 1986, and has been in production since 1989; it was Ginetta's first fully type approved car as distinct from a customer built kit. Based on the G15, it used the running gear of the Ford Fiesta XR2, and was available with either 1.6 or 1.9 litre Ford fuel injection engines.

A convertible was offered from 1990, the same year that the G33 was first shown, a no-compromise sports car that has undoubted appeal for the enthusiast who enjoys the brute power of open air motoring. The G33 has a space frame chassis and all independent suspension and is powered by the Rover 3.9 litre V8 engine.

GT Developments UK
Producers of copies of the Ford GT40 from the mid–1980s, the company also produced copies of the Lamborghini Countach and the Lola 170 Mk III, using V8s supplied by either Chevrolet, Ford or Rover.

The GTD R42 exemplifies the ground effect theory, which has produced a CD of 0.28

At the end of 1993, GT launched its first all-original design, a 300bhp supercar. The GTD R42 has a monocoque chassis and a 4.6 litre quad cam 32 valve V8 engine sourced from the Lincoln Town Car. Its claimed top speed is 292km/h (180+mph), reaching 0–97km/h (0–60mph) in 3.7 seconds.

Healey UK
Donald Healey consolidated his own marque in 1949 with the Healey 100, which was launched at the London Motor Show of 1952. By various agreements, he was able to produce the Austin-Healey with BMC and the Jensen-Healey with Jensen.

The first production car was the 1946 Westland Roadster, a four seater rag top with a 2,443cc Riley four cylinder engine. Capable of 170km/h (105mph), it was the fastest British made four seater at the time. It was later surpassed by the Elliott saloon, capable of 177km/h (110mph). The latter was driven to ninth place in the 1948 *Mille Miglia* by Donald Healey and his son. The Silverstone appeared in 1949, and was to become the basis for the Nash-Healey, the G Type of which appeared in 1951. This was to be the all British version, and was known as the Alvis-Healey. It was the last car in production under the Healey marque which was closed in 1954.

Honda Japan
Following its motorcycle success, Honda built several race cars but then withdrew following an accident. Its first production cars appeared in 1962, but it was not until the Civic model appeared in 1972 that the company finally made a big impression on the market.

Since 1979, Honda had entered into a technology partnership with British Leyland, but this was later severed by Honda in 1994 when Rover announced its share sale to BMW.

By 1984, Honda had become the fifth largest automobile manufacturer in all of North America, with its Accord becoming the most popular model by the end of the decade. Its very first sports car was the S500, which entered production in 1962. A small car with a 531cc four cylinder dohc engine, it was enlarged to 606cc in 1963, when the coupé S600 version was introduced. The S800 followed in 1966, and was capable of a road speed of almost 160km/h (100mph).

Honda's second sports car,

Honda NS-X **(foreground)**

the NS-X, did not appear until 1990, powered by a 2,977cc V6 dohc which was mid-mounted and driven through a five speed gear box.

Intermeccanica Italy/USA
Founded in the 1950s based on blending Italian flair with North American finance, the company was partly involved in the production of IMP, Apollo and Omega cars prior to production under its own name. In 1956, it produced the Italia, an open two seater powered by a V8 Ford 4.7 litre engine. This was the unscheduled result of an abortive attempt to produce a steel bodied TVR Griffith, the Griffith Omega. A convertible version followed in 1968, known as the Torino, which was available with either a 5 or 5.7 litre engine.

The Intermeccanica company was well connected and sold well in Europe via Opel. In 1975, the company moved from Torino to the west coast of the USA, and proceeded to make nostalgic copy cars, which only contributed to its downfall.

Iso Italy

Iso was a motorcycle manufacturer which made its name in the motor industry by creating the first bubble car in 1953. Its first sports car appeared in 1962, before Iso, like so many others, became a victim of the energy crisis. The ensuing financial problems, coupled with labour disputes and the death of the founder, all contributed to the sale of the company but it eventually failed altogether by the mid–1970s.

The Rivolta GT appeared in 1962, styled by Bertone and powered by a 5.4 litre Chevrolet engine. It had a top speed of 228km/h (142mph). A Ghia styled four door version, the Fidia, followed before the Grifo, Iso's most renowned model, appeared in 1965. Styled also by Bertone, it had an engine size option up to a wild 400bhp 7 litre which produced a top speed of 290km/h (180mph). A licensed lightweight version was later made by Bizzarrini as the Strada. Iso's last car, the Lele, had entered production in 1969, also with a Bertone styled body, but with Ford engines.

The 1968 Iso Griffo GL 365 Lusso was powered by a Chevrolet V8 5,359cc 365bhp engine. The Griffo was styled by Bertone, and engineered by Giotto Bizzarini

Jaguar UK

Having started on Swallow sidecars in 1922, William Lyons and William Walmsley sold sports bodies in 1927 and announced their first car, the SS1, in 1931. The company name was altered to Jaguar after the Second World War, and it offered a range of value for money sports cars. In later years, the company acquired Daimler and Coventry Climax, before merging with BMC in 1967. After that, decline set in and the marque was almost discarded before being rescued by John Egan in 1980. Re-marketing the Jaguar as a separate marque, in 1984 he was able successfully to launch the company on the British stock exchange. It was bought by Ford in 1989.

Jaguar's first postwar car was the XK120, with a planned production run of 250, but so successful was this two seater roadster that by the time production ceased in 1954 over 12,000 had been produced. Jaguar had got the style and price right. In 1951, a fixed head coupé was introduced and at the same time, the C-Type was launched. This was intended as a race car able to compete under tougher and faster conditions than the XK120 had been built for. The C-Type met with

The Rolt/Hamilton Jaguar C-Type on its way to victory at Le Mans, 1953

immediate success, winning the 1951 Le Mans race, an achievement repeated in 1953. Production only totalled 58, and of these three street car versions were sold to Farina, Fangio and Ascari, the first three World Champions.

The XK140 appeared in 1954, an XK120 update which was offered in roadster, coupé and drophead coupé versions with a top speed of 210km/h (130mph). In 1957, the more refined XK150 was launched, most of which were produced with a 3,781cc engine.

The D-Type was a pure race model, but it led to the sturdier XKSS, which entered production in 1957, but following a fire at the factory very soon after, the production line was never resumed and only a mere 16 were produced. The XKSJ had

the benefits of D-Type advanced aerodynamics, and was equipped with a 250bhp 3,442cc engine, making it the fastest production car of 1957 with a top speed of 260km/h (160mph). The production variant of the D-Type was the E-Type, which entered production in 1961. The dream car of the early 1960s was sleek, even a little cramped in the cockpit, but under the long bonnet was a 265bhp 3,781cc XK engine, capable of 0–97km/h (0–60mph) in 7.2 seconds and a top speed in excess of 235km/h (145mph). In addition to the popular coupé version, Jaguar also offered a roadster version, and in 1962 introduced a Lightweight E-Type which was in effect a customised model pioneered by John Coombs for special customers with racing

1974 Jaguar E-Type V12 series III roadster

intentions. The 15 that were produced are probably the pick of the E-Types.

The 4.2 E-Type appeared in 1965, with the engine increased to 4,235cc and some refinements made. Basically, however, it took over where the 3.8 had left off, and by 1968 production had reached nearly 17,500. The 2+2 version had a 22.86cm (9in) longer wheelbase but unlike the 4.2 there was no roadster version, only a coupé.

Production ended at the same time as the 4.2's, both giving way to the E-Type 4.2 Series II, which was a way of consolidating all of the modifications introduced since 1961, in addition to complying with new US requirements such as open headlights and raised bumpers. The Series II made way for the Series III in 1971, which introduced the V12 5,343cc 272bhp engine. The previous two seat coupé was dropped as the chassis from the coupé 2+2 was used to house the larger engine. Production ended in 1975, after 15,000 had been produced.

Jaguar had promised an F Type, but it has never appeared. The current XJS, as beautiful and sporty a car as exists, is considered by Jaguar to be a touring car, and as such has won the European Touring Car Championship and the XJ220 is marketed by JaguarSport.

JaguarSport UK
A company jointly owned by Jaguar and TWR was formed in 1989, to market modified Jaguar road cars. In 1989, the XJ220 was announced, and the limited production run of 350 was completely sold out within 48 hours, with the first cars being delivered in October 1993. The XJR–15, also announced in 1990, and intended as a road version of the Le Mans R9R, has yet to appear.

Jensen UK
Jensen marketed its first complete car in 1936, and continued after the Second World War with limited production, until meeting success in the form of the 1967 Interceptor. The company went into liquidation in 1976, but was re-established in 1983 when the company which owned the right to produce spares started marketing the Interceptor again, first as the S4. The S4EFi version was introduced for 1992, with the Chevrolet V8 engine fitted with a Holley twin barrel carburettor with throttle body fuel injection.

The original 1950 Interceptor had had a 4 litre 'six' and was first offered as a convertible with the hard top following a year later. The 541 appeared in 1954, based on a shorter Interceptor chassis and fibreglass body. The 541 was capable of 185km/h (115mph). All round disc brakes became standard in 1956. The 541 R appeared in 1957 and was followed into production by the 541 S in 1961. The 541S was both wider and longer, in addition to being equipped with further added luxuries, making it a first-class GT car.

The first CV8 appeared in 1962 as the Mk I, based on the 541 chassis but with a 6 litre Chrysler V8 which gave it a top speed of 225km/h (140mph). The Mk II appeared in 1964, and the Mk III in 1965. In 1966, Jensen unveiled the new Interceptor at the

Earls Court Motor Show and between 1967 and 1976 over 5,500 were to be produced, initially with a Vignale hatchback body. The convertible was not made available until 1974, when a coupé was also produced. Other versions included the Mk III with a 7.2 litre 284bhp engine and the SP with 330bhp. The Ferguson Formula (FF) was launched at the same time as the Interceptor and was the first four wheel drive with anti lock brakes. The FF's wheelbase was 10.16cm (4in) longer than that of the Interceptor.

Jensen-Healey UK

The coming together of Jensen and Healey in 1969 to produce a Lotus engined sports car made good sense. Unfortunately, the 2 litre dohc engine was always troublesome and the styling of the Jensen-Healey, which was available between 1972 and 1976, left a lot to be desired. It did still manage though to find nearly 11,000 customers, and when not playing up was capable of a top speed of 193km/h (120mph). The Jensen GT appeared briefly in 1975, a sporting estate car with a five speed Getrag gear box.

Lagonda UK

Founded by American Wilbur Gunn, by the mid–1930s Lag-

onda had taken over Bentley's mantle as the number one British sports car by taking the 1935 Le Mans event. After the Second World War, an effort was made to revive the company but it collapsed in 1947, at which time it was purchased by David Brown to ensure the continued provision of an engine for his Aston Martin company. The Lagonda marque was kept separate until 1963, when it virtually disappeared. In 1974, the name was revived as an Aston Martin model name, which has since been dropped.

Immediately after the Second World War, a 2.6 litre model had been introduced, powered by the dohc straight six. This was an expensive car which underwent a minor specification update in 1952 for the Mk II model, but production was halted in 1953 to make way for the 3 litre version. This was available in both two and four door versions and a drophead. In 1961, the Rapide was launched but in a little under three years, only 54 had been sold.

The relaunch of Lagonda in 1974 in the guise of a long wheelbased four door version of the Aston Martin DBS powered by a 5.4 litre V8 was not a success, and only seven were produced before the parent company

The 1989 Lagonda

went into liquidation. In 1976, a new Lagonda was announced and following a number of teething problems delivery began in 1978.

Lamborghini Italy
Ferruccio Lamborghini started a motorbike manufacturing company that was to pass through more hands than any other, based on the concept of offering Italian design style ahead of mechanical competence. It has been a marque that has done little to swell the coffers of any of its owners.

Lamborghini initially built Fiat specials before trying to outstyle Ferrari, but by the 1970s Ferruccio had lost interest when his tractor company was experiencing a tough time and sold the company to Swiss watchmaker Georges-Henri Rosetti. When Rosetti

had watch sales problems in the same decade, he sold the marque on to Leitner, a property developer.

An agreement with BMW to build a production version of the M1 was outlined but never implemented and Leitner sold on together with Rosetti who still held some shares, to the former German racing driver Hubert Hahne and a Dr Neumann. They in turn sold to an American, Zoltan Reti, who wasted no time in putting the company into receivership. At auction in 1981, the company was acquired by the Nimram family, who were making a success of it by the time they sold on in their turn to Chrysler in 1987.

Lamborghini launched its 350GT in 1964, designed as a competitor to the other Italian high rollers of the early 1960s, the Ferrari 400 and the Maserati Sebring. Powered by a 280bhp 3.5 litre dohc V12, the 350GT had a top speed of 240 km/h (150mph) and reputedly superb handling. The car was styled by Franco Scaglione and Touring.

An uprated 320bhp 4 litre engine was installed into 23 cars and from 1966 a new Lamborghini gear box was used. The 400GT arrived in 1966, similar to the 350 but with improved styling by Touring and available as either a 2+2 GT or as an open two seater format. The top speed was 251km/h (156mph) and 0–97km/h (0–60mph) arrived at in 7.5 seconds.

The first Miura appeared at the same time as the 400GT, with the 4 litre engine sited transversely amidships.It was followed by the S model in 1969, with the 375bhp 4 litre engine capable of 290km/h (180mph) and in 1971 by the SV model. A 400GT 2+2 was launched in 1968 under the Islero model name, a sharper looking car styled by Marazzi. It included retractable headlights and all luxury extras. The Islero engine was front mounted and just about managed 275km/h (160mph).

The Espada, Lamborghini's first four seater, was able to utilise the running gear of the Islero but it had a platform chassis and a 10.16cm (4in) longer wheelbase. Body styling was by Bertone. The Jarama was launched in 1970, with a 350bhp front mounted engine at the same time as the Urraco P250, which was designed to take on the Ferrari Dino. Equipped with a 220bhp sohc V8, it had the legs of the Ferrari but was never a match in the showroom.

The Countach LP400 was first shown in 1971 and was greeted with rapturous applause, but it took nearly three years to begin deliveries. Body design

The distinctive four seater
Espada

was by styling guru Marcello Gandini, who was at the time with Bertone, the 4 litre engine was mid-mounted and fixed in line with a five speed gear box ahead of the engine and a drive shaft passing back through the engine sump. The engine produced 375bhp and it could attain a top speed of 275km/h (170mph). The LP400 S appeared in 1978 and the 2S in 1980, with an improved cockpit.

In 1976, the Silhouette was launched, a two seat improved Urraco with a Targa top and a 265bhp 3 litre V8 engine. It was replaced in 1981 by the Jalpa, essentially an improved Silhouette with a 3.5 litre engine.

The following year, the Countach LP400S gave way to the LP500, with a 5,167cc engine, this in turn making way for the LP500 S Quattrovalvole in 1985. With four valves per cylinder, this measured 455bhp and achieved a top speed of 295km/h (183mph). Today production is concentrated on the Diablo, which was unleashed in Monaco in early 1990 and is another Marcello Gandini style statement although Chrysler did meddle a bit; the car carries the *desegno Marcello Gandini* badge. More importantly it has a 5.7 litre V12 fuel injection engine derived from its Countach predecessor.

Lancia Italy

Fabrica Automobile Lancia e Cia was founded in 1906, and in 1922 pioneered the use of integral chassis construction when launching the Lambda. After the Second World War, Lancia found itself, like so many others, underfinanced and in 1955 the Lancia family sold its interests to Carlo Pesenti. From then on, the company concentrated on small cars, but by 1960 was struggling again and by the end of the decade Pesenti was forced to sell to Fiat to cover his enormous debts.

Under Fiat, the Beta was launched but suffered from severe rust problems and Lancia was forced to take back cars. Since then, its sporting activities have concentrated on rallying and together with Martini it has secured the World Rally Championship.

The Aurelia B20 was launched in 1949, and remained in production from 1951 to 1958, during which time over 2,500 were produced, with all independent suspension and a 2 litre ohv V6 engine. The body was styled by Pininfarina, and by 1954 the engine size had been increased to 2.5 litres. On the race tracks, the Aurelia met with marked success, scoring a second place in the 1951 *Mille Miglia* followed by a third position in 1952, a first place in its class at Le Mans and a more than impressive 1, 2, 3 in the *Targa Florio*.

In 1955, the Aurelia B24 was announced in both Spyder and convertible forms. Also styled by Pininfarina, it was powered by a 2,451cc version of the V6 engine. The smaller Appia appeared in 1956, with a 1,098cc ohv V4, but production of both the Series II and Series III models was very limited, with coupé or cabriolet bodies being designed by a variety of Italian names.

The Flaminia Sport and Supersport was the first car under the Carlo Pesenti ownership, and had a 2.5 litre V6 engine and was a two seater styled by Zagato. The Fulvia coupé provided Lancia with its first really big mass produced sports car, with 134,000+ being made between 1965–7. Power was provided by a front mounted V4, which was available in a range from 1,216cc to 2,775cc.

It was superseded in production by the Fulvia Sport which had disc brakes on all four wheels. There was also the Fulvia HF version, produced between 1966–72, which with a tuned engine was prepared for competition. Engine sizes went up to 1,584cc by the time production finished, and these

produced 130bhp and a top speed of 170 km/h (106mph).

The Stratos was the first Fiat Lancia, and was the result of a Bertone concept. Prototypes were produced in 1972 with a mid-mounted 2.4 litre V6 Ferrari Dino engine. In 1975 and 1976, the car won the World Rally Championships and in 1979, in private hands, the Monte Carlo Rally. Homologation made necessary the production of 400 cars, and by the end of production in 1975 Lancia had built 500 of these neat two seat coupés. The top speed for standard 190bhp engines was 230km/h (143mph).

At the same time as Lancia was introducing the Stratos, it was also tooling up for the mass produced Beta coupé, which was a front wheel drive 2+2 with a dohc 1,367cc engine transversely mounted and driven through a five speed gear box. Options included both a 1.6 and a 2 litre engine and from 1975 a spyder version.

The Monte Carlo mid-engined two seat coupé was introduced in 1975. Styled by Pininfarina it was originally intended as a larger version of the Fiat X1/9 and was code named X1/20. The standard engine was a 120bhp 2 litre but it only achieved a paltry top speed of 195km/h (119mph).

Above: *the Lancia Stratos was a winner of 14 championship races and helped Lancia to the 1974 and 1976 championships*

Lister UK

Modified Jaguar XJSs were sold as Lister-Jaguars from 1982, powered by a 6 litre engine and capable of up to 286km/h (178mph). In 1987, the Le Mans model was launched with a 500bhp 7 litre engine developed from the Jaguar V12. The top speed was raised to 320km/h (200mph). At the London Motor Show in October 1993, the Lister Storm was the sensation of the show. An all new British super-car, the first ever completely flat bottomed front engined car with effective underbody and overbody aerodynamics, that apply optimum down force that produces a level of grip usually only found with rear engined cars, the Storm has a six speed gear box and four seats; 0–97km/h (0–60mph) is reached in 4 seconds and the top speed is 320km/h (200mph).

Lotus UK

Lotus was founded by Colin Chapman, whose combination of determination and ability made him one of the leading automobile figures until his death in 1982. Chapman's career has been the subject of many books, but in this volume we can only pay tribute by a mention of the many classic sports cars his company produced. Following his death, Toyota became a minority shareholder before the company was sold to General Motors.

The first production Lotus, the Mk VI, appeared in 1952 and engine options included Ford and MG. In 1954 Colin Chapman

***The near 600bhp Lister Storm
V12 can exceed 320km/h
(200mph)***

drove a Lotus Mk VIII sports
racer to victory at Silverstone
ahead of a Mk VI which finished
in front of the works entered
Porsche 550 driven by Hans
Herrmann to third place.

The Seven Series I appeared
in 1957, after the Mk VI had been
phased out. It was a revamped
Mk VI with a new space frame
and suspension. The choice of
engines now included BMC Series A motors and the most
popular 1,172cc Ford 100E, while
when fitted with the Coventry
Climax engine it was known as
the Super Seven.

The Élite was announced at
the same time as the Seven, and
was the world's first GT with
unit construction in fibreglass.
Over six years, Lotus produced
just under 1,000 units powered
in the main by a Coventry
Climax 1,216cc engine which
produced a top speed of 193km/h
(120mph).

The Seven Series II entered
production in 1960 with a 997cc
Ford 105E engine as basic, but
by the time production ended in
1968, the 105E had been replaced
by the 1.5 litre Ford Kent
engine.

The first Lotus Élan was produced in 1962, and unlike the
unprofitable Élite, the Élan S1
was to prove the making of

Lotus. Introduced as a rag top with pop up headlights, a hard top soon followed, and both were powered by Lotus' own 1,588cc twin cam engine; this gave the Élan a top speed of 185km/h (115mph). The S1 gave way to the S2 in 1964, and in 1966 the S3 appeared; both were minor upgrades.

The Europa S1 appeared in 1966, a mid-engined GT with an odd appearance. It used the 1,470cc Renault 16 engine, but could only manage a top speed

At the end of the 1980s, the Élan had front drive and an Isuzu 1,588cc twin overhead camshaft engine with 16 valves. It was turbocharged and intercooled

of 175km/h (109mph), which was not fast and from 1968, when the Europa was sold into North America, the engine was increased to 1,565cc. A limited edition Seven Series III appeared in 1968. Again this was slightly upgraded, and again available with a variety of engines. This model was the car put into production by Caterham Cars before being copied by many upstart companies.

The improved Europa S2 was available in 1968 though still underpowered. In 1969, the Élan +2 arrived; without doubt this was the best car that I ever owned, and it was then streets ahead of anything else for the money. It gave an excellent

ride, was suitable for a small family, and had the added attraction of being very mean on fuel. The 115bhp engine was instantly responsive. The 130+ 2S introduced in 1971 was capable of a top speed of 193 km/h (120mph) and powering from 0–97km/h (0–60mph) in 7.5 seconds.

The Élan series continued in 1968 with the S4, and the build quality for which Lotus had been criticised in its early years continued to improve. The Élan Sprint version arrived in 1971, with two tone paint work. Later models were fitted with a five speed gear box which had been under development for future Lotus models. The last of the Seven Series, the IV, entered production in 1970 with a new space frame which was both longer and wider than before. The Seven Series finally went out of production at Lotus in 1973.

The Europa Twin Cam made its *début* in 1971, with added power provided by the 105bhp Lotus-Ford Twin-Cam engine, and this, along with some styling modifications, helped to make the Europa a common sense leader in the mid-engined sports car market. In 1974, Chapman announced the Élite S1, a decisive upmarket move. The Élite was a four seater with

a good finish and a new dohc 16 valve 2 litre engine, the Lotus 907.

The first Éclat, the S1, appeared in 1975, and was in effect a fastback Élite. The Éclat was sold in North America as the Lotus Sprint. Although it used the same chassis as the Élite, it was about 45.4kg (100lb) lighter, and had a higher top speed of 207km/h (129mph).

The S1 remained in production until 1980, when it was replaced by the S2.2, which was equipped with a 2.2 litre engine, and a five speed Getrag gear box.

Meanwhile, Lotus had entered production with the Esprit S1, which was launched in 1975, mid-engined and with a wider body. It also shared the same engine and suspension layout as the Élite, but the S1 had a lot of teething troubles and was even slower than the Éclat. This was rectified with the much improved S2 version, which appeared in 1978.

The Esprit S2.2 entered production in 1980, together with the Éclat S2.2, but between all three models the 2.2 litre models sold less than 450 units. The turbocharged version of the Esprit was available from 1980 with a redesigned Type 910 engine, capable of a top speed of 238km/h (148mph), and with 0–

The Lotus Esprit Sport 300, derived from the Lotus Esprit X180R race car, was launched at the 1993 Geneva Motor Show

97km/h (0–60mph) achievable in just over 6 seconds. Top speeds were increased to 245km/h (152mph) with the 1985 model. The Esprit S3 was in production from 1981–7, when it was replaced by the S4, with its improved styling. This contributed towards the new top speeds of 222km/h (138mph) for the standard 2.2 litre engine, and for the Turbo introduced in the same year with 228bhp, 240km/h (150mph). The SE version of 1989 pushed this up to 261.8km/h (162.7mph), and could

accelerate from 0–97km/h (0–60mph) in 4.7 seconds.

The Lotus Excel, which was introduced in 1985 and had been originally sold in 1983 as the Éclat Excel, was softer lined and used Toyota components, including its five speed gear box. Minor modifications have since been introduced.

In 1989, Lotus reintroduced the Élan, powered by a transversely mounted 1,588cc 16 valve four cylinder engine, which powered it to a top speed of 195km/h (121mph).

Marcos UK

Founded in 1959 by Jem **Mar**sh and Frank **Cos**tin, its first car was of timber and plywood con-

57

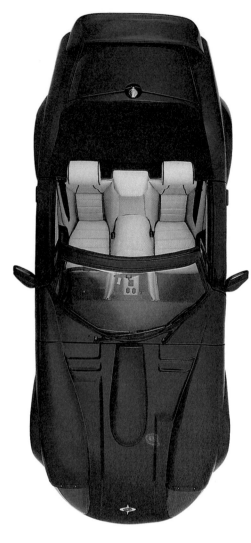

An unusual view of the Marcos Mantara coupé

struction. Costin was soon to leave the company, and by 1968 the wooden monocoque had been abandoned so as to enable Marcos to break into the big North American market. Ford engines were used initially, but these were replaced by the straight six Volvo unit which was both heavy and expensive, and the company subsequently went into liquidation in 1971. The Marcos was reborn in 1981, when Jem Marsh Performance Cars was established.

The first Marcos was the gull wing GT coupé, which remained in production from 1960 to 1963. Power was provided by a Ford four cylinder, initially the 105E. The GT was followed by the 1800 which, with its fibreglass body, was to create the Marcos reputation. It used the 1,800cc Volvo engine, retained the plywood monocoque and was capable of 186km/h (116mph). In 1966 the 1800 was replaced by the 1500, which used a Ford engine, as did the 1600 that replaced it in 1966.

In 1965, the Mini-Marcos was introduced, using a fibreglass body/monocoque and Mini components. Following the collapse of Marcos, the production of the Mini-Marcos was taken over by Rob Walker who sold it to D & H Fibreglass Developments in 1975.

The gull wing car of 1961/2 used a Ford engine

The 1966 Mini Marcos was the only British car to finish the Le Mans 24-hour Race

The first Marcos to appear without the plywood monocoque was the 3 litre of 1969, powered by a 140bhp Ford V6 engine. A 2.5 litre was also produced, using a Triumph TR6 engine, which appeared in 1971 after the large engined 2 litre had been introduced, with its 85bhp Ford V4.

The four seat Marcos Mantis was launched in 1970, a coupé with a tubular chassis and powered by the Triumph TR6 engine, producing a top speed of 200km/h (125mph). The low swept nosed Mantis was in production when Marcos folded, and is often blamed for its demise.

Since 1981, Marcos has offered Ford engined kits and in 1984 introduced the Mantula, with a Rover V8 engine, capable of a respectable 220km/h (137mph). The Spyder followed in 1986, a convertible version of the Man-

tula powered by a 3.9 litre fuel injected Rover engine with a top speed of 240km/h (150mph).

Maserati Italy

It was the racing cars of Maserati in the years between the two World Wars that made its reputation, but it was always an underfinanced company and had to struggle to compete with the first division companies. In 1938, the company was sold to the Orsi industrial group, and postwar the founding Maserati brothers departed to form OSCA to pursue their racing interests. Maserati also concentrated on Formula 1 until 1957, when it began to produce cars that competed in style and mystique with Ferrari.

In 1968, a co-operative venture was agreed between Maserati and Citroën, which led to Citroën taking a majority share holding. Then

Citroën itself became part of Peugeot in 1975, and Maserati was saved from dissolution by Alejandro de Tomaso. Chrysler bought Maserati in 1984, and in 1990, in a continued selling off of his empire, de Tomaso sold 49% of Maserati to Fiat.

The first postwar Maserati road car was the A6/1500 powered by a 1,488cc sohc straight six. A top speed of 153k/mh (95mph) was claimed for the Pininfarina styled GT, which was phased out of production in 1950 to make way for the A6G. This was based on the chassis of the A6, but was powered by the 1,954cc engine which delivered 100bhp and was capable of a top speed of 160km/h (100mph).

The A6G 2000 went into production in 1954 and raised the top speed to 190km/h (118mph). It was followed by the 3500 GT and GTI in 1957, the same year in which Maserati won the Formula 1 World Championship. The 3,486cc dohc straight six engine drove through a four speed ZF gear box and the model was available as a 2+2 hard top styled by Touring or a Vignale styled convertible.

The 5000 GT was introduced in 1959, powered by a 5 litre engine in the 3500 GT chassis; this was now essentially a 2+2 coupé, although a convertible was also produced. A short wheelbase 3500 GTI was produced in 1962, and marketed as the Sebring, with a Michelotti (Vignale) styled 2+2 body and a top speed of 215km/h (135mph).

A second edition appeared in 1965, with a 245bhp 3,694cc engine which increased the maximum speed to 240km/h (150mph). In 1963, Maserati launched the Mistrale, which was very much a Sebring with a short chassis, but lighter and quicker, and this remained in production until 1970.

The first new sports car to use the V8 engine was the Mexico, launched in 1965. It was a four seater with a live rear axle and a five speed ZF gear box. The 4.2 litre engine boasted a maximum speed of 240km/h (150mph), while the 4.7, which became available in 1967, was quicker still. The better styled (Ghia) Ghibli made its appearance in 1966, with a shorter wheelbase than the Mexico; it was available as both a coupé and an open top, from 1969.

A 4.9 litre engine was fitted in 1970, which produced 335bhp. In the same year that the Ghibli was launched, there also came the Indy. A 2+2 replacing the Sebring, it had a 4.1 litre engine which was replaced in 1970 by a 4.7 litre, producing a top speed of 250km/h (156mph). The en-

A 1972 4.7 litre Maserati Tipo 115 Ghibli SS Spyder

gine size was enlarged again in 1973 to 4.9 litres.

Ital Design produced the body style for the Bora, which was introduced in 1971, a mid-engined car powered by a 4.7 litre engine which was also increased to 4.9 litres in 1975, giving a top speed of 260km/h (160mph).

The Merak entered production in 1972 as a counter to the Ferrari Dino, powered by a 3 litre V6 in a Bora chassis. This was always an under performer, with 0–97km/h (0–60mph) in a very modest 8.2 seconds. Next into production was the front engined Khamsin, which replaced the Ghibli and was styled by Bertone, who also supplied the unitary steel con-

struction. Power was provided by a 320bhp 4.9 litre which raised a top speed of 240km/h (150mph).

The Quattroporte had been launched in 1963, and was not a true sports car; the Quattroporte II, launched in 1975, managed a production run of five before Maserati went to de Tomaso after its split from Citroën. After that, De Tomaso began to market a new range of Maserati which sold by marque name and not marque ingenuity. The Kylami, introduced in 1977, was a De Tomaso Longchamps by another name, but powered by a 4.1 litre V8 Maserati rather than a Ford.

The new Quattroporte III was launched in 1977, an Ital Design styled stretched Kylami. It was originally offered with a 4.1 litre engine but with a 4.9 litre option, the latter becoming standard from 1985. In 1987, it was renamed the Royale, and the specification was more luxurious. Today, the Maserati range includes the 2 litre Spyder with a top speed of 225km/h (140mph), the Karif, a 2+2 coupé equipped with a 2.8 litre engine, and the Shamal, a disappointing coupé introduced for 1990 with a 3,217cc engine, and a six speed Getrag gear box.

The 1994 S Shamal model has a top speed of 270km/h (167.7mph) from its 3,217cc V8, which produces 326bhp with two turbochargers and clocks 0–100km/h (0–62.5mph) in 5.3 seconds

Matra France

Matra was launched on the auto scene in 1964, with the Matra-Bonnet, then a Formula 3 and an F2 car followed. In 1969, Simca took over the company, and so Matra became part of Chrysler. In the 1968–9 season Jackie Stewart became World Champion driving a Cosworth-Matra. This was followed by Le Mans victories in 1972, 1973 and 1974, and in 1978 the company was bought by Peugeot. In 1983, Renault took a controlling interest and has since produced the Matra designed Renault Espace at the factory.

Matra's first sports car, a fibreglass bodied 2+2, was the M530A launched in 1967. Powered by a 1.7 litre Ford V4,

its top speed was no more than 153km/h (95mph). In 1973, the Bagheera replaced the M530A and production reached over 47,500 units before this was replaced by the Murena in 1980. The Bagheera was originally marketed as the Talbot-Matra.

From 1977, there was also the S model with a larger 1,442cc engine giving top speeds of 177km/h (110mph). The Bagheera was a three seat sports car with two seats squashed in to the right of the driver. It begat the Murena in 1983, with the same layout and cockpit but with a new body shape and a choice of two engines, a 1.6 litre or 2.2 litre Chrysler, which would yield a top speed of 195km/h (121mph).

Mazda Japan

Founded in 1920, the company began producing motorcycles in 1931, and then three wheeled trucks. Postwar production of trucks was started in 1945, and in 1960 the first Mazda car was produced. In 1961, Mazda signed an agreement with NSU to produce the Wankel engine, since when car production, including that of Wankel engined vehicles, has steadily progressed with Ford purchasing a 25% stake in the company to develop markets and to build the Mazda 323.

Mazda's first sports car was the 110S coupé launched in 1967, a front Wankel engined car with a normal capacity of 1,964cc and a top speed of 185km/h (115mph). There was a gap between 1972 and 1978, before the RX–7 appeared, a twin rotor Wankel engine which had a normal capacity of 2,292cc. However, Mazda appeared to have got it right, and production reached over 500,000 units throughout the range. In 1986, Mazda introduced the RX–7 with a new chassis and the 2,616cc engine that had made its appearance in the American GSS-SE version of the original RX–7 in 1984. The British version was powered by a normally aspirated 2,254cc engine which gave a top speed of 206km/h (128mph) or a turbocharged 238km/h (148mph).

During the past few years the Mazda range has been extended to include the popular MX–5 or Miata, a smaller Lotus Élan sized sports car with a 1,598cc dohc four valve engine capable of a top speed of 183km/h (114mph).

Overleaf, top left: *the front drive MX–3*
Top right: *MX–5 convertible*
Centre: *the MX–6 2 + 2*
Bottom: *Mazda image maker, the unique rotary engined RX–7*

McLaren UK

Set up by New Zealand racing driver Bruce McLaren shortly before his death in 1970, the company had built its first supercar by 1969. The M6GT, a spin off from the Can-Am M6B, was a monocoque construction designed by Robin Herd and Gordon Coppuck, with power provided by a Chevrolet V8. Production of the M6GT was halted after McLaren's death, but a new company, McLaren International, announced the three seat F1 in 1990 and unveiled the stunning supercar at Monaco in 1992, since when deliveries have begun.

The McLaren F1 is probably the sports car of the 1990s

Mercedes-Benz Germany

The founding father of the car industry, its early days are well documented. After the Second World War, the country was struggling to return to its feet and there was not the money readily available to the general populace for buying Mercedes cars, but by 1950 production was back up to over 100 units daily.

In 1952, Mercedes-Benz was back participating in motor racing, banned until 1950 for German companies, with a works team of 300SL Coupés. Unhappy with the pressures, it withdrew from racing for over 30 years following a fatal crash at Le Mans, and consequently the company's sports cars, unlike its saloon car division,

have not been a major force in postwar production.

The 300SL Coupé was introduced in 1954 following the racing model. Notable for its gull wing doors, power was supplied by a sohc 2,996cc straight six inclined to the side and fuel injected. The top speed was 225km/h (140mph). At the same time as the 300 was introduced, Mercedes launched the 190SL, of which over 25,000 were to be produced by the time production ceased in 1963. Powered by a four cylinder sohc 1,897cc engine, it had a top speed of 170km/h (105mph).

When production of the 300SL Coupé ceased in 1957, it was replaced by the 300SL Roadster. More spacious than the Coupé, this was a definite improvement on its predecessor.

From 1963 through to 1971, Mercedes produced the 230SL, 250SL and 280SL, the first of which was powered by a 2,308cc engine, and was capable of a top speed of 190km/h (120mph) when the 250SL was introduced in 1966. It was the first of the Mercedes sports cars to have all round disc brakes, and the

The original 300SL coupé, created in 1952 and now in the Mercedes museum

1960s six cylinder 300SL convertible

2,496cc engine was a halfway house before the 280SL arrived the following year. This had a 2,778cc 180bhp engine. From 1969, the ZF five speed gear box became an option.

Between 1972–89 followed the illustrious long line of SL and SLC models which were known as the R107 series, and ranged from the 350SL of 1970 with a 3,499cc V8 engine to the 560SL, which went out of production in 1989 and was powered by a 5,547cc V8.

In 1989, Mercedes introduced new 300SL and 500SL models, open top two seat convertibles. These new models had it all, beautifully styled aerodynamic bodies, built in safety features, an exceptional degree of comfort and finish and a 4,973cc V8 engine in the top of the range model that produced 322bhp and had a top speed of 252km/h (157mph) with a 0–97km/h (0–60mph) time under 6 seconds.

MG UK

Cecil Kimber founded Morris Garages (MG) in 1924, and in the 1930s the marque came to the fore with a series of wins in international racing events, culminating in its sale to Morris Motors in 1935. After the Second World War, models starting with the TC were successfully exported to the USA, but it was not long before MG found itself part of the British Motor Corporation and eventually it fell foul of boardroom decisions that reduced the marque to a badge on 'performance editions' of standard saloons. However in 1993 a new MG sports car was announced and there is reasonable confidence for believing that it may be in production by 1995.

The MG that first captured the hearts of North America was the TC, which entered production in 1945. Powered by a 54bhp 1,250cc with a top speed of only 120km/h (75mph) and not available with left hand drive, the export orders still enabled production to reach 10,000 units before it was replaced at the end of 1949 with the TD.

By now, MG had learnt its marketing lessons and the vast majority of the nearly 30,000 TDs produced between 1950–3 were left hand drive. The TD also handled better than the

TC, but the top speed was still only 130km/h (80mph). The TF made its *début* in 1953 with a 1,250cc engine, the 1,500cc being available from 1954; and although the body line was sleeker it was by now an ageing design and sales figures started to dip.

The new shape MG finally appeared in 1955 in the form of the A/A Coupé, which had MG's first rigid chassis, and a 72bhp 1,492cc series B BMC engine. In 1958, the MGA Twin Cam was launched with disc brakes all round and a top speed of 177 km/h (110mph), but there were problems with the engine and MG soon dropped the model. The MGA 1600 appeared in 1959, and the Mk II in 1961, with an 86bhp 1,622cc engine which was capable of a speed of 160km/h (100mph) but 0–97km/h (0–60 mph) still took 13.7 seconds.

The Midget Mk I was actually an MG badge on an Austin-Healey Sprite Mk II. In 1962 the engine was enlarged from 948cc to 1,098cc but it was still slow. Production lasted from 1961–4. Much more successful was the MGB Roadster, which appeared in 1962, derived from the MGA. It was equipped with disc

The MGB advertisement that epitomised the marque in Great Britain

brakes only on the front and a 1,798cc engine, which powered the car to 166km/h (103mph) and 0–97km/h (0–60mph) in 12.2 seconds.

The Midget Mk II, a rebadged Sprite Mk III, appeared in 1964 and in 1965 yet another MGB appeared. Slightly cheaper, slightly heavier and slightly slower, the MGB GT still sold at the rate of 200 units per week. The Midget continued to be produced; from 1966 the Mk III with 1,275cc engine, from 1969 the Mk IV when a new trim and new wheels were introduced, and finally the Mk V, with large US type plastic bumpers added, and a 1,493cc Triumph Spitfire engine and gear box. This increased the top speed to the magic 160km/h (100mph). Unfortunately, the Midget Mk

An MG TD Sports two-seater from 1951

V passed from production in 1979, the last of MG's sports cars.

Meanwhile, in 1967, MG launched the B/BGT Mk II, which sold well despite growing competition from Japan in the North American market, where MG lacked an engine with any power which conformed to US emission laws. The MGC and CGT were launched in 1969, both with the largest MG engine to date, a 3 litre 145bhp unit shared with the Austin 3 litre saloon. Sadly, this was too heavy for the MGC and resulted in poor handling even though top speeds of 193km/h (120mph) were possible.

In 1973 a decent engine was

finally used, the Rover V8, which was fitted into the MGB to produce the B GT V8 with a top speed of 200km/h (124mph) and reduced the 0–97km/h (0–60mph) time down to 8.6 seconds. The car, however, was not marketed in the USA and although enthusiasts had waited patiently for the right power unit, the car was now becoming expensive for a model that had been around for over a decade.

In 1974 both the MG Midget Mk V with its large bumpers and the last MGB and MGB GT entered production. The Mk II will remain a collectors' piece for some time to come; despite the fact that early models did not handle too well, it was the last model in production.

During the early 1990s rumours grew of a new MG, until in late 1993 it was finally announced. A brand-new MG Midget two seat comes to the market by the end of 1995; code named PR3, it is aimed at the lower end of the market, a pure soft top with the engine mounted transversely behind the cabin, driving the rear wheels.

Mitsubishi Japan
A shipping company originally founded in 1870, its initial car based on a Fiat design appeared in 1917. Its first domestically

designed cars did not appear until 1959, and early models were all with engines of under 500cc. In 1979, the car division of what was by now a huge corporation became independent and in 1981 Chrysler bought a 35% holding.

The company moved into the higher performance market with turbocharged engines which powered its saloons and the Eclipse coupé. In 1989 it announced the 3000 GT, its first sports car, which was available the following year. This is marketed in North America as the Dodge Stealth, and in Japan as the Starion GTO. The 3000GT is a 2+2 coupé with four wheel drive, four wheel steering, four wheel ABS braking, and four wheel electronically controlled suspension.

Morgan UK
Founded in 1910, the company started by building three wheelers, designing its 4/4 in 1936. After the Second World War the 4/4 design was put into production and in 1946 the first car appeared, with its vintage chassis and 1,267cc Standard engine. The Plus Four replaced the 4/4 in 1951, with a longer wheelbase which was designed to take the four cylinder 2,088cc Standard Vanguard engine. The top speed was 138km/h

(86mph) and 0–97km/h (0–60mph) was achieved in 17.9 seconds.

A new body style was introduced in 1953 with extended front wings and a curved radiator grille. The Plus Four with the TR engine entered production in 1954. The 90bhp 1,991cc Triumph TR2 engine was upgraded during the production life of the Plus Four, which lasted until 1969. The TR2 engine gave a top speed of 154km/h (96mph) while later engines provided top speeds in excess of 170km /h (105mph).

The 4/4 was revived in 1955 as the Series II, powered by the Ford side valve 1,172cc 100E engine. The Series III, which appeared in 1960, had a wider body and was powered by a 54bhp 997cc ohv Ford 105E engine which was the unit used in the Anglia. A 2+2 version of this was also offered.

During the 1960s Morgan, in conjunction with the Chris Lawrence company Lawrence-tune, produced about ten cars per year with tuned TR engines which were capable of a top speed of about 193km/h (120mph). The 4/4 continued in 1962 with the Series IV, which introduced front discs to the model, which was powered by a 1,340cc Ford engine. The Series V followed in 1963, this time powered by the 1,498cc engine from the Ford Cortina GT.

The Plus Four Plus made its *début* in 1963. It was a coupé on a Plus Four chassis and powered by a TR4 engine. The fibreglass body was an odd shape, but the top speed was a creditable 177km/h (110mph). The 1967 model of the 4/4 was powered by the 1,599cc Ford Kent engine and was the only +2 Morgan then in production.

From 1982, the Ford unit was replaced by a 1,585cc dohc Fiat engine. The Plus Four, which reappeared in 1988, was powered by the 2 litre Rover dohc M16 unit, and had a top speed of 175km/h (109mph) and 0–97km/h (0–60mph) was down to 7.7 seconds.

The Plus Eight was introduced in 1968, and remains in production today, originally with a 3.5 litre Rover V8 and now with a 3.9 litre fuel injected 187bhp engine driven through a five speed gear box. The 4/4, which actually signifies 4 wheels and 4 cylinders, remains in production and is now available with an 1,800cc dohc, while the Plus Four now uses a Fiat 2 litre 16 valve twin cam.

The top of the range Morgan Plus Eight has been in continuous production since 1969

MVS France

The dream of stylist Gérard Godfroy and engineer Claude Poiraud was to create a luxury French sports car to take on the rivals of Ferrari and Porsche. Established in 1984, the Manufacture de Voitures de Sport (MVS) company is now 90% owned by Primwest France and 10% by Omnium Europe, and is a partner in the Venturi-Larrouse Formula 1 team. The Venturi made its *début* in 1991. Moulded in composite materials, the aerodynamically effective body sits on a strong rigid steel monocoque. Turbocharged 2.5 or 2.9 litre versions of the PRV V6 are mounted amidships and the cabriolet version features a two piece 'Transcoupé' roof, which allows four positions between saloon and full open motoring.

Nissan Japan

In the 1930s, the Tobatau Immo company acquired another called DAT, which produced small engined light cars. In 1933, it formed the Nissan Motor Company, which soon started exporting Datsuns. Larger cars were later produced, together with lorries, both of which carried the Nissan badge. After the Second World War, Nissan continued production of its prewar model range, until 1952 when it started to introduce Austin designed vehicles, made by Nissan under licence.

By 1960, when Nissan started to export again, it was the second largest automobile maker in Japan, and in 1961 it formed a subsidiary manufacturing plant in Mexico; today there are also plants in Australia, the UK and the USA. The Datsun name was dropped in 1983 for UK models.

The first Nissan sports car was the D–3, which appeared in 1952, but which was a prewar design and was powered by a side valve 860cc four cylinder unit. A 2+2 convertible appeared in 1959, the first Nissan Fairlady, the S211 used the chassis of the D–3 and a fibreglass body. Power came from an 1,189cc four cylinder ohv engine which gave a top speed of 128km/h (80mph).

In 1961 the Fairlady sports car appeared, initially being available with a 1,488cc engine. The 1,596cc engined model was available from 1964, and was equipped with front disc brakes. The top of the range was the Datsun 2000, which arrived in 1967 with a new sohc 1,982cc four cylinder engine.

The Fairlady line was replaced in 1969 with the Fairlady Z series, better known as the

Datsun 240 Z. This was the car that established Nissan in North America, where it began to outsell the British imports. The 240 Z was powered by an sohc 2.4 litre straight six driven through a five speed gear box. A three speed and automatic were both options, and the top speed was 200km/h (125mph).

In 1963 the 260 Z, with a 2,565cc engine, appeared and in 1975 the 2,753cc engined 2+2 280 Z was introduced. In 1978, the 280 ZX replaced the 280 Z; using the same engine as the 280 Z, it had disc brakes all round and was longer and wider than the original Fairlady Z range. It was offered as a two seat or a 2+2, and the interior comfort was also improved.

A 280 ZX turbo was offered in 1981, with a top speed of 210km/h (130mph), reaching 0–97km/h (0–60mph) in 7.4 seconds. Today's model range includes the

The 170bhp Datsun 240Z

200 SX/Silvia, which was introduced in 1988, and launched in the UK in 1989. With rear wheel drive and a four cylinder in line 1.8 litre engine with four valves per cylinder, Nissan built in many safety extras but still had to limit the top speed of this positive drive 2+2 coupé to 225km/h (140mph).

Nissan's other current sports model is the 300 ZX, which was introduced in 1989, and was regarded as Japan's first real super sports car. Today's fourth generation Z car is packed with features which include four wheel steering, anti lock brakes, viscous limited slip differential and a pair of removable roof panels. The 24 valve twin turbo V6 develops 278bhp and has a top speed of 250km/h (155mph) with 0–97km/h (0–60mph) in 5.6 seconds.

Pontiac USA

A separate division of General Motors created in 1926, Pontiac came to the fore in the 1960s under the guiding hand of John Delorean, with a series of muscle cars.

In 1984, Pontiac launched the Fiero, with a mid-mounted 2.5 litre four cylinder engine that gave a top speed of 170km/h (105mph), and reached 0–97km/h (0–60mph) in 8.5 seconds. A 2,837cc V6 engine was offered as an option from 1984. In 1985, Pontiac introduced the fastback bodied GT, and in 1986 a five speed gear box.

Pontiac's own idea of a sports car, the Fiero

Porsche Germany

The endeavours of Dr Ferdinand Porsche, the man who designed the people's car, the VW Beetle, are well documented. The 356 was the great man's first achievement, the first Porsche car to appear, in 1949; it was a lighter and aerodynamically styled Beetle, powered by the flat four air cooled 1,131cc engine which had been tuned to give 40bhp and a top speed of 135km/h (84mph). The engine size was reduced in 1950 to 1,086cc, and one of these powered the 356 to win the 1100 class at Le Mans in 1951. In the same year, a cabriolet version was offered, and also the split screen was replaced by a single

1956 Porsche 356A 1600S coupé

one piece windscreen.

Engine options followed, and included 1,287cc, 1,290cc, and 1,488cc; a lightweight America speedster version appeared too, just prior to production being switched in 1955 to the 356A. This was an upgraded version with an improved dashboard. The basic model was powered by a 1,600cc engine, and the 356A also became available as a hard top coupé or speedster rag top.

The move to the 356B took place in 1959, with a much more exaggerated Beetle body design, which now incorporated raised headlights and a revised bonnet plus wheel trims. The 1.6 litre engine was retained with 130bhp being delivered for

the Carrera 2 version, which was introduced in 1960. The last 356 series entered production in 1963, and lasted until 1965. The 356C was a continuation of Porsche's development and the 356 finally was given disc brakes all round, together with improved suspension. The C, despite being available in a variety of bodies, was only available with a 1,600cc engine, which could be either 75bhp or 95bhp.

Porsche's second sports car model to appear was the 904 GTS in 1963, powered by a 2 litre dohc flat four which was positioned amidships, unlike the 356, which was rear engined. The body was fibreglass and Porsche produced just 100 examples in order to homologate the model for racing purposes. It did not disappoint, winning the 1964 *Targa Florio* and finishing second the following year in the Monte Carlo Rally.

The classic 911 appeared in 1964, a rear engined car with MacPherson struts at the front and a 130bhp 1,991cc flat six air cooled engine. The Targa top did not appear until 1967.

The 912 model, which appeared in 1976, was very much a downgraded 911, with a 90bhp 1,582cc flat four and a lower quality of interior fit. There was a break in production between 1969 and 1976, with the reintroduced model, the 912E, aimed at the American market and with fuel injection.

Porsche launched the more powerful 911, the 911S, in 1966, with a high compression engine of 160bhp. With fuel injection available from 1968, this was increased to 170bhp and provided a top speed of 220km/h (137mph). In 1969, the engine size was increased to 2.2 litres, and this was replaced with a 2.4 litre unit in 1971.

The 2 litre 911T was introduced in 1967; very much the smaller brother, it was originally powered by a 110bhp 2 litre, upped to 2.2 litres in 1967 and to 2.4 litres in 1971, but even that was only tuned to 130bhp with a top speed of 177km/h (110mph).

Other 911 models include the 911E, introduced in 1968, a touring car with fuel injection and from 1969 with a 2.2 litre engine, upped to 2.4 litres in 1971.

The 911 Carrera, a name reserved by Porsche for its finest models, appeared in 1972, with a 2.7 litre flat six engine. In 1975 the 911 Turbo followed, with a four speed gear box, a top speed of 251km/h (156mph) and 0–97km/h (0–60mph) in 5.2 seconds capability. The interior finish of the Turbo was more luxurious, with leather seats and the body had an engine lid aerofoil, which had first appeared on the 911 Carrera.

The Turbo's engine size was increased in 1977 to 3.3 litres, with 330bhp and a top speed of 260km/h (160mph). A Targa version appeared in 1987, and a five speed gear box in 1989. In 1993, Porsche celebrated 30 years of the 911 with a new 911 Carrera, which was unveiled at the Frankfurt Motor Show in September 1993. This new model had a completely newly designed chassis with a multi link lightweight strut axle (LSA) rear axle to give improved active driving safety, ABS braking system with optional control programming and a 3.6 litre engine producing 272bhp through a six speed gear box.

The 911 had been rationalised in 1978 to a Turbo and an SC model, with a 3 litre engine, servo assisted brakes were introduced in 1979 and a cabriolet model was added to the range in 1982. In 1984, the engine was altered to a 3.2 litre sohc flat six, and the above mentioned SC model grew into the Carrera. The Sports Equipment (SE) model appeared the next year, still with a normally aspirated engine and a top speed of 232km/h (144mph). In 1989, the 911 underwent serious alteration and with four wheel drive became the Carrera 4, which was powered by a 3.6 litre flat six. Later that year, a two wheel drive version, the Carrera 2, became available, just slightly quicker than the Carrera 4 at 254km/h (158mph).

The 924 had been originally designed for Volkswagen, and depended heavily on the Volkswagen/Audi parts bin. The first 924s were made by Audi, but were marketed as Porsches. The 924S appeared in 1985, and the competition 924 Carrera GT arrived at about the same time. Group 4 homologation dictated the building of 400 of these, with 210bhp turbocharged engines; the GTR was the racer and the GTS was the rally version.

By 1977, Porsche had already introduced the 928 series, similar to the 924 in looks, but with a fuel injected sohc 4.5 litre V8 it was much smoother and also its roadholding was faultless. The top speed was 228km/h (142mph) but for the S version of 1979, this was increased to 245km/h (152mph). In 1984, the Series 2 model took over, with a four speed automatic gear box and anti lock brakes.

The Series 3 was powered by a 5 litre engine, but this was only available in the USA, and had Bosch LH-Jetronic fuel injection. The Series 4 appeared in 1986, also with the 5 litre unit, and the GT in 1989. Today's 928 GTS is powered by a 5.4 litre four cam 32 valve alloy V8 with power raised to 340bhp at 5,700rpm. The current model also has sharper rear styling.

A turbocharged 924 appeared in 1978, and was considered a stop gap between the lower performing 924s and the arrival in 1982 of the 944. The latter used Porsche's 2.5 litre in line, water cooled four in place of the 924's Audi engine. In 1982 the 944 Lux appeared, in 1986 the 944S and 944 Turbo. In 1988, a cabriolet version was launched and the engine size upped to 2.7 litres for the base model which was then capable of a top speed of 219km/h (136mph). The S was eventually replaced by the S2,

Cutaway drawing of the Porsche 2.5 litre model 924S

Four cylinder in line light alloy water cooled engine with two counterbalance shafts to minimise vibration, a digital fuel injection and ignition system, and 2.5 litre capacity with a 160bhp (DIN) output

Dual circuit servo-assisted braking system with floating calipers and internally ventilated front discs; rack and pinion steering; light alloy wishbones with double acting hydraulic shock absorbers and MacPherson strut suspension. The 6J × 15 road wheels are light alloy with 195/65 VR 15 tyres and 20mm (0.78in) anti-roll bar

The all-galvanised, steel construction aerodynamic body shape results in a low drag coefficient, $Cd = 0.33$. The frontal area is 1.76m², maximum speed 222.6km/h (137mph),

from 0–100km/h (0–62.5mph) in 8.2 seconds; the rear spoiler on the tailgate reduces lift at high speeds, and its glass enhances all-round visibility

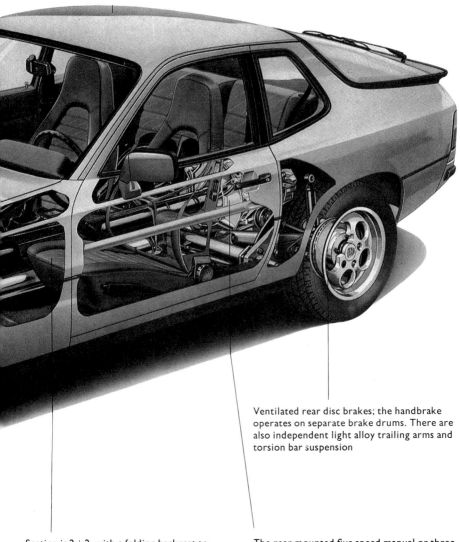

Ventilated rear disc brakes; the handbrake operates on separate brake drums. There are also independent light alloy trailing arms and torsion bar suspension

Seating is 2 + 2, with a folding backrest to increase luggage capacity. The ergonomically optimised seating design is available in fabric, leather and leatherette combinations

The rear mounted five speed manual or three speed automatic gearbox is connected to the engine by a transaxle driveline system. The rear wheels are independently sprung

A 1985 944 Turbo, which was introduced that year

Right: 968 CS coupé of 1993, evolved from the 944

with a top speed of 240km/h (149mph) from its 3 litre engine. The 944 Turbo was introduced in 1985, originally powered by the 2.5 litre sohc engine, and by 1991 there was a cabriolet version available.

Between 1987 and 1988, 200 units of the model 959 were produced, that was first intended for Group B homologation. Porsche was too late; the Group was abandoned and the 959 had become a limited edition super-car. Power was provided by a water cooled 2.9 litre flat six,

with twin turbochargers, which delivered 405bhp and pushed the top speed beyond 305km/h (190mph). Reaching 0–97km/h (0–60mph) was a blink at 3.5 seconds.

The 944 has evolved into the 968, with better handling, and it is a better driving car than the 944 with near zero lift aerodynamics in both the coupé and the cabriolet versions. VarioCum electric hydraulic valve timing has now been added also to the dohc four cylinder engine that delivers 240bhp.

Reliant UK

Founded in 1935, the company began as a constructor of vans, not making its first lightweight saloon until 1953. The first sports model was the result of co-operation with Autocars Ltd of Israel, to which Reliant was selling fibreglass bodies. The model was sold in the UK as the Reliant Sabre, from 1961.

The Scimitar GTE established the company's reputation but when production of this ended in 1986, to be replaced by the SSI, sales slumped and the company closed in 1990.

The Sabre model of 1961 was powered by the 1,703cc Ford Consul engine, and had an all synchromesh four speed ZF gear box. Most of all Sabres (75%) went to Israel, about one third of these in kit form.

The Sabre Six SE2S was a much improved model, which appeared in 1962. Power was provided by the six cylinder 2,553cc Ford Zephyr engine, and the top speed was a respectable 177km/h (110mph), but sales were meagre. The Scimitar SE4A appeared in 1964, rights to a 2+2 coupé body having been bought from the Ogle design studio. This was married to the Sabre Six running gear.

The SE4B appeared in 1966, powered by a new Ford 3 litre V6, which provided a top speed of 195km/h (121mph) and the following year the SE4C was launched, with a 2.5 litre unit. The Scimitar GTE SE5 came next in 1968, an Ogle redesign as a sporting estate car which retained the Ford 3 litre V6.

I consider myself fortunate to have been the owner for a number of years of Reliant's next model, the GTE SE6, which was launched in 1975. This was 10.16cm (4in) longer and 7.62cm (3in) wider than the previous SE5, and was the ideal sporting estate. The SE6a continued some improvements, and from 1979 the power was provided by a 2.8 litre Ford V6.

The lighter SE6b appeared in 1982, and was the last Scimitar GTE, but in 1986 the model was dropped and the rights were later acquired by Middlebridge Scimitar Ltd, but it also went into receivership, in 1990.

In 1980, Reliant launched the Scimitar GTE SE8b, a four seater rag top which had also been styled by Ogle. The Scimitar SSI appeared in 1984, a two seat rag top quite different in appearance to earlier Scimitar models. It was also much slower, being powered by a 1.3 litre engine only, and even when the 1.6 litre unit was made available, the SSI did not impress. In 1986, the SSI 1800 Ti made amends for the SSI's sluggishness with a turbocharged 1.8 litre engine which had come from the Nissan Silvia, and now provided the SSI with a top speed of 202km/h (126mph) and an 0–97km/h (0–60mph) time of 6.9 seconds.

A restyled SSI appeared in 1990 as the SST 1800 Ti model, with a much improved panel fit but a 1.4 litre engine which was definitely short of power and was the last of the line for Reliant.

Renault France
Founded by Louis Renault in 1898, the company holds the distinction of winning the first ever *Grand Prix*, in 1906. By 1913

it had grown to become the biggest motor manufacturer in France, as it still is. In 1945, the company was nationalised, following the death of Louis Renault in October 1944. The company continued to expand and in the 1970s returned to motor racing after an absence of over 60 years. It entered Formula 1 in 1977, since when it has been a major supplier of engines for other Formula 1 teams.

Renault's first sports car did not appear until 1983, the mid-engined 5 Turbo 2. This was a two seat coupé which was powered by a 1,297cc four cylinder engine and used much of the Renault 5, including its gear box and platform. The top speed for the standard model, but not that marketed by Renault Alpine, was 200km/h (124mph).

Saab Sweden

Saab was founded in 1937 with a great deal of State backing to build military aircraft. It did so with a successful combination of flair and advanced technology. In 1950 its first car appeared, instantly heralding Saab's rallying success. Its only sports car to date is the Sonnet II, which was launched in 1966 with an 841cc three cylinder two stroke engine. In 1967, Saab switched to a more powerful 1.5 litre Ford V4, and in 1970 the fibreglass bodied Sonnet III took over. This had a 1.7 litre engine fitted from 1971, but production ceased in 1974 owing to falling orders.

Simca France

Simca was formed in 1934, with the purpose of making Fiats under licence in France. After the Second World War, the first Simca designed car, the Aronde, appeared in 1951. During the 1950s, Simca bought out fellow manufacturers Talbot and Ford France, and in 1963 sold a controlling interest in the company to Chrysler. Simca was renamed first in 1976, as Chrysler, then in 1979 as Talbot, following the Peugeot takeover.

The first postwar sports car was the 1948 Eight Sport, with a Pininfarina styled body. These were built by Facel, and the Fiat 1100 running gear was built by Simca. The model ceased production in 1956, when it was replaced by the Aronde Océane, a two seater that was offered as either a coupé or a convertible. The Bertone styled 1000 Coupé appeared in 1962, a 2+2 which had a 52bhp four cylinder engine capable of a top speed of 145km/h (90mph). The 1000 Coupé was phased out in 1967, to be replaced by the 1200S, which had a similar shape but a 1,204cc engine. Production ceased in 1971.

Subaru Japan
A maker of utility vehicles, Subaru has finally packed its knowledge into a luxury sports coupé, the SVX. This is powered by a 3.3 litre flat six which has 24 valves and four camshafts, at the front of the car, driving all four wheels through a four speed automatic transmission with both economy and power modes. The top speed is 232km/h (144mph) and 0–97km/h (0–60 mph) is reached in a modest 8.7 seconds.

Suzuki Japan
Another Japanese manufacturer to enter the sports car market, but unlike Subaru, which entered at the luxury end, Suzuki has launched with a small car, the Cappuccino, which is being acclaimed worldwide as the ultimate small sports car since its launch at the 1993 London Motor Show. A unique blend of styling, driver and passenger appeal and technological leadership, the Cappuccino provides ultimate sports car performance and enjoyment in the purist tradition. Dimensionally, it is almost identical to the MG Midget.

Toyota Japan
The Toyota Motor Company was formed in 1937, and began by building General Motors models under licence. It took a long time for production and sales to get back to an even keel after the Second World War, but when they did they moved progressively up the world rankings until Toyota arrived in the top three of world producers.

Postwar sports car production was not prolific; it launched the S800 in 1965, which was powered by a 790cc flat twin with a top speed of 156km/h (97mph). The production run ended in 1969, by which time the 2000GT was being produced. This was a two seat coupé conceived by Yamaha, powered by a dohc 1,998cc straight six with a five speed manual gear box. The top speed was 220km/h (137mph), and 0–97km/h (0–60mph) was attained in 8.4 seconds.

Toyota's big breakthrough into the sports car market came in 1984, in the shape of the MR2, which was available with either a 1,453cc or a 1,587cc engine and with many other options which combined to give a top speed range of between 170 to 210km/h (106 to 130mph). This original MR2 remained in production for just five years

The mid-engined 1993 Toyota MR2GT model

before being replaced by a completely redesigned MR2 in 1989. This time, the engine size was fixed at 1,998cc but the range of bhp produced – up to 222bhp for the turbocharged version – meant that the top speed could be as high as 240km/h (150mph).

The latest generation of MR2 continues the original mid-engine concept, but in 1992 was reworked to take larger alloy wheels with specially developed Yokohama tyres; the power steering gives better feel, grip and control, and the standard 2 litre four cylinder in

line fuel injection engine with four valves per cylinder provides a very economical 13.45km/l (38 miles per Imp gal/31 miles per US gal).

Toyota's mainstream sporting model, the Celica, is now a highly equipped front drive GT with a twin cam 16 valve 2 litre engine which has 158bhp available and a top speed of 220km/h (137mph). The GT Four, with permanent four wheel drive. and a turbo engine, is capable of topping 230km/h (143mph). The turbo system now has a water cooled intercooler.

Toyota's top model now, however, is the Supra, which went on sale in the UK in August 1993, and packages the entire Toyota equipment inventory into a rear drive coupé of phenomenal performance; 0–97km/h (0–60mph) in 4.9 seconds, 250km/h (155mph) (limited from over 289km/h/180mph), 326bhp from a sequentially turbocharged twin 3 litre six cylinder engine. Pioneering lateral G-sensing ABS, switchable traction control and either six speed manual or four speed automatic transmission make the Supra a wow.

Triumph UK

Triumph created its early reputation with the production of motorcycles and although it did produce a three wheeler in 1903, its first four wheeler came in 1923, and a separate new Triumph Motor Company, was formed in 1930. In mid-1936, the Triumph Motor Company became independent of the motorcycle company, and went on to gain a reputation for middle range sports cars. However, just before the Second World War, the Company went into receivership and the assets were subsequently sold to Standard. In 1961, Standard-Triumph merged with BMC. Triumph thus became a founder member of British Leyland (BL) in 1968, and under BL Triumph lost its sports car market and Triumph

sports car production ceased in 1981.

Triumph launched its Roadster 18TR model in 1946, a two seat version of the Triumph 1800 saloon, with a Standard ohv 1,776cc engine. In 1948, the TRA took over the production line, and was powered by a 2,088cc Vanguard engine. A two seat version of the Standard Vanguard was launched in 1950 as the TR-X, but was immediately withdrawn after only three had been made. The TR2 did reach production in 1953, with a 1,991cc Vanguard engine and a top speed of 165km/h (103mph) and Triumph finally broke into the American market.

The TR3, which followed in 1955, was an improved version of the TR2, and in 1956 front disc brakes were introduced. Further improvements were made in 1957, with the TR3A. The TR4 arrived in 1961, a re-bodied TR3; while for North America, Triumph released the TR3B. Both had a top speed of 164km/h (102mph). A limited special edition was produced as a 2+2 coupé with a fibreglass body, and sold under the model name of Dove.

The Triumph Spitfire I was launched in 1962, based on the Herald, with a Herald 12/50+ 1,147cc four cylinder engine which produced a top speed of 145km/h (90mph). The Mk I gave way to the Mk II in 1955.

Triumph's next model was the GT6, a coupé bodied Spitfire which appeared in 1966, powered by a 2 litre straight six Vitesse engine, and was beset with handling problems, which Triumph quickly overcame to launch the GT6 Mk II in 1968. This became the GT6+ in North America.

The TR5 PI appeared in 1967, still very much based on the TR4 but with a 2.5 litre straight six engine. The model was sold in North America as the TR250, with a top speed of 172km/h (107mph), which was 21km/h (13mph) below the version that was on sale in other markets.

The Spitfire received a new 1,296cc engine in 1967, and became the Mk III. This meant an improvement in the top speed to 160km/h (100mph), with 0–97km/h (0–60mph) attainable in 13.6 seconds. Sales received a considerable boost.

Below: *the 1977 works rallying TR7 V8 coupé*

The TR6 went into production in 1969, a re-bodied TR5. Time to reach 0–97km/h (0–60mph) was reduced to 8.2 seconds, and the top speed was raised to 191km/h (119mph). The next Spitfire on stream was the IV, which appeared in 1970. This had both a new nose and a new tail, together with a new instrument layout. However, US emission control laws bit too heavily into the Spitfire's continued success rate, and Triumph fought back by introducing the 1.5 litre engine in 1973.

In 1970 the final GT6, the MK III, appeared and remained in production until 1973, but it was also the victim of the US laws; while the UK version had a top speed of 180km/h (112mph), the US version could manage only 154km/h (95mph). The falling off of US sales was the reason for the Mk III's short production life.

The 2+2 Stag arrived in 1970, with the choice of either rag top or a hard top. The engine was a 3 litre V8, derived from the Dolomite, and had a top speed of

186km/h (116mph). The last Spitfire was the 1500, introduced in 1974. It sold just short of 100,000 units before being phased out in 1980. Power was provided by a 1,493cc 71bhp engine. The 1500 was followed into production by the new TR7, Triumph's first sports car for over a decade.

It first appeared in only a hard top version, the rag top not being introduced until 1979. A Triumph 1,998cc 105bhp engine was used, but the top speed was only 177km/h (110mph). The last Triumph, the TR8, was a re-engined TR7, with a Rover 3.5 litre V8, but production came to a halt within a very short time after only about 2,500 had been built, most of which found their way to North America.

TVR UK
Founded in 1947 as Trevcar Motors, its first car was an Alvis special in 1948. The following year, the name was altered to TVR Engineering, and its first car was a bits conglomerate, but it did sell and enabled the company to progress onto production of kit cars, using fibreglass bodies and a TVR chassis. In 1965, the company was sold, and changed its name again, this time to TVR Engineering Ltd, since when it has progressed to become the biggest independent British sports car producer.

The first TVR sports car was the Grantura I, which appeared in 1957, a notchback fibreglass bodied coupé which could be fitted with a variety of engines but most usually a 1,172cc side valve Ford unit. The Grantura Mk II followed in 1960, and the Ford engine gave way in popularity to the 80bhp 1,588cc MGA engine. At the same time, the Mk IIA was produced, with the 86bhp 1,622cc MGA engine. The company went into liquidation in 1962, but was quickly back in production under new management with the Mk III Grantura, which was a much improved model with an all new chassis but the same 1,622cc MGA engine as standard, which provided a top speed of 160km/h (100mph).

The Griffith 200 was the result of Jack Griffith installing a 4,727cc Ford V8 into Mk III bodies and chassis supplied by TVR. They were badged in America and sold as Griffiths. The Griffith 400 was based on the Mk IV chassis. Unfortunately the car was rather an uncontrollable mess, and received nothing but criticism. Meanwhile, the Grantura continued to sell steadily in the UK, with the Mk IV being introduced in 1964.

The Vixen took over from the Grantura and was much the same, except for a new bonnet scoop. By now, the company was under the ownership of Arthur Lilley and the TVR models became more refined as the quality of finish improved. The Vixen was powered by a 1,599cc Ford engine. A longer wheelbase Vixen, the S2, had appeared in 1968, and in 1970 the S3, with a 93bhp engine.

Fascinated by what Griffith had tried to do, Lilley attempted to get the formula right with the Tuscan V8 model. It was not well received but undeterred, he produced a longer wheelbased V8SE, with a smoother body, but this still failed to attract. However, the Tuscan was now in production for the home market as the V6, with a 136bhp 3 litre Ford V6 engine, which gave a top speed of 200km/h (125mph).

The 1300 was launched in 1971, as an economy model equipped with a 63bhp Triumph Spitfire engine; this was another TVR that attracted few buyers. A more successful model was in production alongside it, however. The 2500 (a reference to the 2.5 litre Triumph straight six engine) was sourced from the TR6. Both the 1300 and the 2500 models were out of production in 1972, at which time TVR went into production with four others.

The Vixen S4, which was to be the last of the Vixen range, used the new M chassis, but the same Vixen body. The second 1972 model was the 2500M, and though using the M chassis and an updated Grantura body, it was a development of previous 2500 models which had had the Triumph TR6 engine. The 3000M also entered production, and was similar to the 2500M but with a 3 litre Ford V6 and a top speed of 210km/h (130mph). The fourth of the new 1972 models was the 1600M, which heralded the end of TVR's reliance on kit car production, going out as VAT came in in 1973. It was powered by Ford's 1,588cc cross flow GT engine.

In 1976, a hatchback 3000M was launched as the Taimar, with a 3 litre Ford engine and a convertible version, TVR's first, was available from 1978. A turbo version was introduced in 1975 of the 3000M, the first British turbocharged production car, and its top speed was upped to 224km/h (139mph). Turbo versions of the Taimar and of the convertible followed.

The Tasmin arrived in 1980; based on the M chassis, it had a 10.16cm (4in) longer wheelbase than the Grantura. It was launched initially as a two seat

coupé, but the 2+2 was not far off, along with a convertible, both originally powered by a fuel injected Ford 2.8 litre V6. A cheaper version used the Ford 2 litre Pinto engine.

The engine was switched to a Rover V8 following Peter Wheeler's takeover in 1982, and in 1984 the model name was dropped and the car remained in production as the 280i (Ford engined) and the 350i (Rover engined). When the Rover 3.9 litre engine was employed, the model was marketed as the 390SE. Its top speed was 270 km/h (143mph), reaching 0–97 km/h (0–60mph) in 5.7 seconds.

The 420SEAC was launched in 1986, using Kevlar and carbon fibre in the car's construction and powered by a 300bhp 4.2 litre engine. It was capable of a top speed in excess of 240km/h (150mph) and was thus the fastest TVR to date. The Ford engine was discarded in 1987 in favour of the Rover 3.5, 4 and 4.5 litre units.

The 400SE appeared in 1988, with a revised body shape and the four litre engine; it was joined in 1989 by the 450SE and the two models looked set for a long life.

In 1986, TVR had launched a more traditional model, the S model, which was a two seat convertible with a 2.8 litre Ford V6 engine and five speed Ford gear box. The engine was uprated to 2.9 litres in 1988, when it became the S2. There were also S2C models with twin catalytic convertors, and S3/S3C with longer doors. The top speed for the S is 227 km/h (141mph).

In 1989, TVR's first convertible 2+2 was launched, as the Speed Eight, with a 3,950cc Rover V8 and a top speed of 232km/h (144mph). However, there were initial delays and the car did not enter production until 1991, by which time TVR had shown the Griffith with an entirely new body and a 3.9 litre 240bhp engine and a top speed of 238km/h (148mph).

Currently the TVR range is more exciting than ever, with the dynamic S series model which is now in its fourth generation, the latest evolution being the S4C. The Griffith 500, which features a 5 litre 320bhp TVR Power V8, was launched in 1993, and has revised suspension and larger ventilated disc brakes both front and rear, to cope with the extra power and stunning acceleration. The Chimaera and the Chimaera 2+2 followed on using the same chassis, drive train and suspension as the Griffith, but with the option of a 4 or 4.3 litre V8 engine. The Chimaera was launched in 1993.

Left: *the 1994 TVR Griffith 500*

Below: *another TVR 1994 model is the superb V8 engined S series*

Volkswagen Germany

Hitler laid the foundation stone for the Volkeswagenwerk in 1938, but production was cut short after just a few cars had been built. Major Ivan Hirst was able to restart production in 1945 with a mixture of army and civilian personnel, and the factory was returned to German administration in 1948, at which time Dr Ferdinand Porsche's Beetle was still the basis of production.

Since then, the VW Beetle chassis has been the starting point for a large number of the sports car projects throughout the world, and as such merits Volkswagen's entry here. Volkswagen's only claim to a factory produced sports car is the Karmann Ghia, which was first launched in 1955 as a 2+2 coupé. It also used the Beetle running gear, and 1,192cc engine. The top speed was 124km/h (77mph). A cabriolet appeared later, and in 1963 the larger engined 1500S model became available.

Volkswagen-Porsche Germany

Links between the two companies had remained strong from their foundation, and in 1969 a mid-engined sports car was launched under both badges. The 914S was originally powered by the VW 411 flat four

Right: *a special Volkswagen-Porsche 914 built for Ferdinand Piëch*

engine, and was indeed more VW than Porsche. It also did more for VW's image than for that of Porsche, whose buyers considered the VW badge an indignity.

Other versions included the 914/6, made between 1969 and 1972, and the 914SC, from 1972 to 1975; also the 916, planned to utilise the Porsche fuel injected 911S engine, which produced a top speed of 233km/h (145mph). Porsche halted production of the latter after just 20 units, in order to avoid the marketing of effectively a Porsche-badged VW model, in the 'purebred' range.

Volvo Sweden

Established in 1926, the Volvo marque has become synonymous with safety in its most boring form. It is therefore surprising to discover sports car production spanned a number of years, even though sales were never dramatic. Its first foray into the market was made in 1956, with the two seater P1900, using the PV444 saloon suspension and 1.4 litre engine. Production was stopped in the same year, and it was not until 1961 that Volvo tried again.

94

This model was the P1800, which was powered by a 1,778cc engine and until 1964 was assembled by Jensen. The engine size was increased when assembly was switched to Sweden in 1967, and the top speed was improved to 185km/h (115mph). In 1971, Volvo launched the 1800ES, which was a sporting estate version of the coupé. At the same time engine power was increased again to 120bhp for a larger 1,958cc engine.

Volvo's final sports car, the 480ES, was introduced in 1986.

Power came from a 1.7 litre engine which gave 106bhp when injected, and 120bhp with turbo. The turbo's top speed was 193km/h (120mph).

Zita UK
The last entry in this slim volume was based on the popular combination of a fibreglass body fitted to a VW Beetle floor plan and marketed as the Zita ZS. The company appeared in 1971 and yet again like too many aspiring car makers, failed very quickly.

ACKNOWLEDGEMENTS

Superlaunch Ltd thank the many manufacturers who have generously contributed information and illustrations, without whose support this book would not have been possible.

Below: *the Mondial 8*